Contents

Page references in these Notes are to the Pan Classics
edition of *The Return of the Native* but as references
are also given to particular chapters, the Notes may be
used with any edition of the book.

Preface by the general editor

The intention throughout this study aid is to stimulate and guide, to encourage your involvement in the book, and to develop informed responses and a sure understanding of the main details.

Brodie's Notes provide a clear outline of the play or novel's plot, followed by act, scene, or chapter summaries and/or commentaries. These are designed to emphasize the most important literary and factual details. Poems, stories or non-fiction texts combine brief summary with critical commentary on individual aspects or common features of the genre being examined. Textual notes define what is difficult or obscure and emphasize literary qualities. Revision questions are set at appropriate points to test your ability to appreciate the prescribed book and to write accurately and relevantly about it.

In addition, each of these Notes includes a critical appreciation of the author's art. This covers such major elements as characterization, style, structure, setting and themes. Poems are examined technically – rhyme, rhythm, for instance. In fact, any important aspect of the prescribed work will be evaluated. The aim is to send you back to the text you are studying.

Each study aid concludes with a series of general questions which require a detailed knowledge of the book: some of these questions may invite comparison with other books, some will be suitable for coursework exercises, and some could be adapted to work you are doing on another book or books. Each study aid has been adapted to meet the needs of the current examination requirements. They provide a basic, individual and imaginative response to the work being studied, and it is hoped that they will stimulate you to acquire disciplined reading habits and critical fluency.

Graham Handley 1991

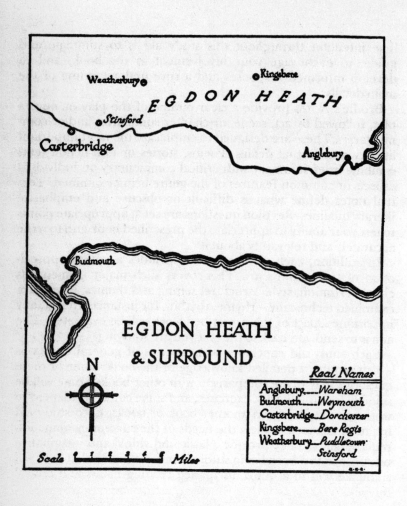

Weatherbury

Kingsbere

EGDON HEATH

Stinsford

Casterbridge

Anglebury

Budmouth

EGDON HEATH
& SURROUND

N

Real Names

Anglebury_____Wareham
Budmouth_____Weymouth
Casterbridge_Dorchester
Kingsbere_____Bere Regis
Weatherbury_Puddletown·
_____Stinsford

Scale |__|__|__|__|__| Miles

The author and his work

Thomas Hardy was born on 2 June 1840, the eldest child of a master mason (he would nowadays be called a builder) of the hamlet of Upper Bockhampton, in the parish of Stinsford near Dorchester. The house was on the edge of heathland that stretches from Puddletown to Wareham; indeed the heath came right down to the back door, and the young boy must have had an intimate knowledge of it. It appears in *The Return of the Native* as Blooms-End. Hardy's father was comfortably off but unambitious; his mother was a woman of driving ambition, an omnivorous reader who taught Thomas to read when he was three, and had decided ideas that her children should do well in the world. The portrait of Mrs Yeobright in the novel is generally considered to be derived from her, as she too has ambitions that Clym shall 'do well'. Mr Hardy's business was a good one; at one time he employed no fewer than fifteen men, including his neighbour the 'tranter', who carried all his building materials. Conditions in the neighbourhood were much as Hardy describes them in *Under the Greenwood Tree* (1872) and in *The Return of the Native*. The secluded and self-contained community was as yet unaffected by the machine age (though the railway came to Dorchester when Hardy was seven years old); *The Return of the Native* looks back to that time.

As a child Hardy was precocious but delicate, and he was eight before he started school. First he went to the village school at Lower Bockhampton (which was to appear as Fancy Day's school in *Under the Greenwood Tree*) and a year later to a private school in Dorchester. He worked hard and became a good all-rounder in his studies, showing a particular aptitude for Latin. He was a shy boy and very earnest. In his leisure time his father taught him to play the violin and prepare manuscript music for himself. One of his first presents from his father was a toy accordion. His father was a fiddler in the west gallery of Stinsford Church, one very much in demand at country festivals. Hardy's father, grandfather and great-grandfather had all been in the choir and were master-masons at Stinsford; it was a coveted hereditary honour in the family.

We read in *The Return of the Native* of Mr Yeobright that:

Whenever a club walked he'd play the clarinet in the band that marched before 'em as if he'd never touched anything but a clarinet all his life. And then, when they got to the church-door, he'd throw down the clarinet, mount the gallery, snatch up the bass-viol, and rozum away as if he'd never played anything but a bass-viol.

Here we are probably reading a description of Hardy's own grandfather. After school and in the holidays father often took the boy with him when he was playing at weddings in the neighbourhood, and the pictures of the various village gatherings – the play of St George, the party at East Egdon and the maypole scene at the end of the book – are all derived from these functions.

Mention has already been made of the ambitions of Hardy's mother. It was she who provided him with the foundation of his wide reading – at a time when there were few books written explicitly for children – and under her guidance he read Dryden's *Virgil*, Dr Johnson's *Rasselas*, and works by Shakespeare, Scott, Dumas, Milton, and various popular novelists of the day. He had extra lessons in French and German; he was an active member of Stinsford church, taught at Sunday School and learned much of the church services and the Bible by heart. There is plenty of evidence of Hardy's knowledge of the Bible in *The Return of the Native* – not the well-known biblical episodes only but obscure Old Testament episodes too. Mrs Hardy was a good singer and used to sing old ballads to her son. The atmosphere of books and music and a countryside that was full of history – Rainbarrow was only a quarter of a mile away and the Roman road from Silchester to Dorchester passed close by – all fed his growing imagination.

While the boy was wondering if his knowledge of Latin would lead to a career in the Church, in 1856 his father arranged for him to become a pupil of John Hicks, a Dorchester ecclesiastical architect, whom he had met in business when working to his designs. Young Thomas pursued his studies when working hours were over, and taught himself Greek as well as improving his Latin. Speaking of his life as a young man of twenty, Hardy wrote that 'the professional life, the scholar's life, and the rustic life combined in the twenty-four hours of the day'. His intellect and imagination flourished and blossomed with contacts such as John Hicks, a near-neighbour William Barnes, dialect poet and philosopher, and other scholarly acquaintances and fine craftsmen. To this period belong a few poems, but they were not published. His work as a student architect was always his first concern.

Thus in 1862 he went to London as 'a young Gothic draughtsman who could restore and design churches and rectory houses', working in the office of A. W. Blomfield, a leading London architect. Straightaway in the same year he won the RIBA (Royal Institute of British Architects) essay prize, and the success of his entry was in no small measure due to its literary quality. He followed this up by winning the Institute's prize and medal the next year. Some eight years later, together with another architect, he had his designs for schools accepted in a competition arranged by the London School Board. His first published work was in *Chambers' Journal* in March 1865 – 'How I Built Myself a House', a gently ironical piece, easily written.

Hardy took the opportunity of widening his artistic interests in the cultural wealth of the capital. He visited the museums, galleries and libraries; he studied painting especially, and references to art and artists are frequently to be found throughout his novels. He read widely and deeply in all manner of subjects, including science and philosophy: the works of Charles Darwin (1809–82), T. H. Huxley (1825–95), Leslie Stephen (1832–1904), J. S. Mill (1806–73) and Herbert Spencer (1820–1903), whose unorthodoxy had an immense influence in liberating thought from traditionally accepted beliefs. His reading had a profound effect on the young man; by the age of twenty-seven he had become an agnostic. His difficulties were intellectual but the clash with his upbringing was a real one, and the emotions aroused by the church's influence on him as a child were such that he continued to go to church to the end of his life.

Throughout this time Hardy was becoming progressively more interested in literature – in the great classics and in the work of little known writers found in the exciting contemporary publications of the 1860s. He read where he wished and did not follow a course, as at a university; but all his life he was to regret that he had not had the opportunities of his friend Horace Moule, who went to Cambridge. It was to make Hardy all the more determined to show that he had not lost anything in the process, which meant that many of his novels, including *The Return of the Native*, show an anxiety to display the author's breadth of knowledge.

In 1867 Hardy returned to Dorchester as an assistant to his old principal Mr Hicks. It was now, back at home, that he started to write fiction. His first effort was not accepted; the second, *Desperate Remedies*, rejected by Macmillan (later to be his publishers), was accepted only at his own risk by a lesser-known house (1871). He lost on it financially, and the novel was remaindered, but he had the satisfaction of seeing his work in print. Despite its experimental nature *Desperate Remedies* bears what we recognize as the Hardy stamp, with its rather morbid episodes, its church and churchyard scenes, a certain air of fantasy and some emotional force — all of which were intensified and improved in later novels.

If *Desperate Remedies* was not an unqualified success, it enabled Hardy to discover where his true strength lay — in the description of the Dorset countryside and people. He set about writing another novel, and after revisiting Bockhampton, was able to finish it, and to get it accepted by Tinsley Brothers at their own risk. *Under the Greenwood Tree* was published in 1872 and Hardy received £30 for the copyright. He did not feel confident enough to publish under his own name, partly because the *Spectator* review of *Desperate Remedies* had welcomed an anonymity that would save disgrace to the family name. Further, if he let his employers know that he spent his time writing novels, and unsuccessful ones at that, it might affect his business reputation. He need not have feared. *Under the Greenwood Tree*, if not an immediate success, was no failure; neither in England nor in America the following year.

But the secret had leaked out in the publishing world. One day Hardy received a letter from the new editor of the *Cornhill Magazine*, saying that he had much admired the freshness of *Under the Greenwood Tree*, and enquiring if he would write a serial for the *Cornhill*. He was too busy at that moment writing *A Pair of Blue Eyes* for *Tinsley's Magazine*, but promised his next work. The result was his first great novel, *Far From the Madding Crowd*, which appeared in the *Cornhill* in 1874. He now felt quite safe in giving up work as an architect for good, and on his royalties from the book he married a Cornishwoman of his own age, Emma Lavinia Gifford, whom he had met over four years before while doing architectural work on a church. It was she who, in 1871, when he was needing encouragement, urged him to stick to literature. Hardy's retiring nature is shown in his quiet wedding; only two witnesses were present, and neither of those was from his family.

In 1876 the newly married couple moved into their first house: Riverside Villa, Sturminster Newton, about twenty miles from Dorchester. From there he was able to take his wife to see his mother at Bockhampton. The meeting was not a success, as the temperaments of the two women clashed violently. In this clash we can see the foundation for the relationship between Eustacia and Mrs Yeobright, which was to be the central conflict in *The Return of the Native*. Hardy always kept a detailed notebook, and the experiences of these years are duly echoed in his next novel – even to the tour of the battlefield at Waterloo that he and Emma made in 1876. *The Return of the Native* was written during the stay at Sturminster Newton, and Hardy later called it 'our happiest time' – particularly because he was looking back on the heath at Bockhampton as he remembered it from his early childhood. For this he needed to distance himself from the actual scene, and it means that distances and even the size of the heath-croppers seem greater than they really are.

Emma, however, was ambitious; she wanted to live in London, and her husband's literary success made her feel that she should be able to do so. They therefore moved in March 1878 to Upper Tooting, near Wandsworth Common. By this time Hardy's initial affection for Emma had begun to cool, for her outlook was basically suburban and middle-class, while his imagination was ready to admit to his novels material of which she could not approve. It is probable that the strains in his marriage were one element in an outlook that became increasingly pessimistic: when *The Return of the Native* was written this process had not yet advanced so far as it was destined to do later, but we can nevertheless see it foreshadowed in the fatalistic resignation of Clym Yeobright.

After *The Return of the Native* Hardy's reputation was secure, and he went from success to success (though not all his novels met with popular approval). The most famous of his novels – *The Mayor of Casterbridge* (1886), *The Woodlanders* (1887), *Tess of the D'Urbervilles* (1891), and *Jude the Obscure* (1894) have in common an outlook that is fundamentally tragic.

The last, quite out of keeping with Victorian sentiment, was attacked so fiercely by the general public and by Emma that

Hardy determined to write no more novels. Instead at his house Max Gate on the edge of Dorchester, which had been finished in 1885, he returned to poetry, with such success that nowadays he is thought of as one of the great poets of his age.

In 1912 Hardy's wife died. In 1914 he married Miss Florence Dugdale, an author of children's stories. She was an Enfield woman of Dorset stock who had acted as secretary to him for some time, had helped him with his writing when his eyes were bad, and had looked up material for him in the reading room of the British Museum. There was nearly forty years' difference in age between them, but her love, devotion, admiration and unceasing care made his last years supremely happy. She became one of his first biographers, though there is strong evidence that the book she wrote was written in collaboration with him and that together they concealed everything he did not wish to become known. Hardy was an intensely private man though he described himself as aloof rather than shy. His pleasures were simple, and not until he became too infirm to cycle would he buy a car.

Acknowledged as the greatest living English novelist, Hardy had reached this position with no regular school or university education, but now three universities were happy to honour him (and themselves) by awarding him the honorary degree of D.Litt. Hardy tried to ward off would-be admirers; could never be persuaded to talk about himself; shrank from making speeches. The honour he appreciated most was the Freedom of Dorchester – more even than the Order of Merit with which he was invested in the same year (1910). Hardy's last public appearance was in 1927, when he laid the foundation stone of the new buildings of Dorchester Grammar School, of which he had been a governor for many years. His love of music continued to the end, and his violin and 'cello always stood in a corner by the bookcase in his study. His works were constantly reprinted, and when he died on 11 January 1928 he left a fortune of nearly £100,000.

The irony that pervades much of Hardy's work was given a dramatic twist after his death. It was decided that the man who had never sought fame should be buried in Westminster Abbey; there were quarrels over precedence for tickets, and the Prime Minister was among the illustrious who bore the pall. The avowed agnostic was buried in England's national shrine.

The body was cremated and the ashes interred in Poets' Corner, next to Dickens's grave, with a spadeful of Dorset earth thrown over. But his heart was carried back to Stinsford, where it was buried in the grave of his first wife.

Plot, source and setting

Plot

Thomasin and Clym Yeobright are niece and son respectively of Mrs Yeobright, who owns a house on the edge of Egdon Heath; Mrs Yeobright secretly hopes that they will marry. Two years before the novel opens, Thomasin had been sought in marriage by a wandering reddleman, but he had been turned down by Mrs Yeobright because his social status was not high enough. He never ceases, however, to be interested in Thomasin and to hope that the situation may change. She, meanwhile, has been captivated by a failed engineer called Damon Wildeve who keeps a local inn. After various interruptions, caused by difficulties over licences, and by his own attraction to a magnetic beauty named Eustacia Vye, Wildeve marries Thomasin, partly to spite Eustacia.

Clym in the meantime has returned from Paris, where he has been a diamond merchant, with the intention of giving up that occupation and starting a school for the benefit of the heath-folk. He and Eustacia meet, are mutually attracted, and marry.

Wildeve is torn between his wife and Eustacia; Clym between his wife and his mother (who dies under distressing circumstances soon after their marriage). Neither couple has much in common, but the marriage of Clym and Eustacia is the stormier, as their basic incompatibility is compounded by her ambition to leave the heath for the supposed delights of Paris, while he wishes only to stay on the heath. All this is acted out against a background of Clym's failing sight.

Eventually Eustacia, while half-intending to elope with Wildeve, falls into a weir and is drowned; he too is drowned while trying to to save her. Eighteen months later the reddleman Diggory Venn (now a dairyman) marries Thomasin; Clym, who had himself thought of proposing to Thomasin, becomes an itinerant preacher in the area of the heath.

Source

The most important source is the heath, which Hardy had known since his earliest years and which is the backdrop to the whole novel. Many of the incidents that appear in the story are derived from fact, though details have been altered and made to fit their new setting: among these are the Christmas mumming at Mrs Yeobright's; Christian Cantle's dicing, which gives him a prize he does not want; and the scene where Venn gambles with Wildeve for the guineas (based on a story that had been told about Hardy's own grandfather).

Hardy's own reading is another important ingredient. The ideas that Clym brings back from Paris, and wishes to impart to the people of the heath, are largely derived from the work of the French philosopher Auguste Comte, which Hardy had been studying for a number of years. The structure of the novel and several other details are derived from Greek tragedy and the works of Aristotle and his theories of tragedy. The passages on the bird and insect life of the heath have their origins in various works of natural history, all of which reappear in the author's notebooks.

All these and many others are fused together by Hardy's imagination into the novel we know. What is perhaps not so generally known is that the first fifteen chapters as originally submitted to the *Cornhill Magazine* were significantly different from the final work. Thomasin, for instance, was originally Mrs Yeobright's daughter and Clym's sister. The novel opens with her seeking refuge in Diggory Venn's caravan because the marriage licence is invalid; originally Thomasin was to have lived with Wildeve for a week before discovering that the marriage ceremony had been illegal. Eustacia in the first draft had been more of a witch than she is in the finished version. *The Return of the Native* is therefore something of a compromise, and the modifications Hardy made to the story he had first conceived were often undertaken in response to the demands of society's conventions – particularly those created by serial publication.

Setting

The setting of *The Return of the Native* is perhaps its most powerful single ingredient. It dominates the novel more than does the setting of any other Hardy novel, and it conjures up in the reader an image of a large area of country. In the opening of the book Hardy himself refers to the setting as a 'trackless waste'. Yet the modern visitor will look in vain for this huge heath. The reason is to a considerable degree the fault of twentieth-century man, who has planted conifers right down to Hardy's birthplace at Bockhampton and has turned the eastern part of the heath into a range for testing tanks; indeed one has to search for relics of the heath as it used to be. Yet this is not the whole story. In his preface to an edition of the novel published in 1895, Hardy wrote:

Under the general name of 'Egdon Heath', which has been given to the sombre scene of the story, are united or typified heaths of various real names, to the number of at least a dozen; these being virtually one in character and aspect, though their original unity, or partial unity, is now somewhat disguised by intrusive strips and slices brought under the plough with varying degrees of success, or planted to woodland.

The indication is therefore clear that the Egdon of the novel is a distillation of the essence of all these heaths. The name Hardy took, slightly modified, was from the vast Iron Age hill fort of Eggardon, on the other side of Dorchester. But Egdon contains all that he remembered of the heath that came to the door of the cottage where he was born – and Hardy remembered a great deal. We read too that 'the date at which the following events are assumed to have occurred may be set down as between 1840 and 1850'; that is, the time when Hardy himself first knew it. His intermittent absences from 1862 onwards had been enough to sharpen that recollection, and the brief visit home with his new wife came at just the right time to give it form.

Egdon is shown in all its seasons. The novel opens in November because the sombre qualities of that month are to be its dominating mood. The way each character reacts to the surrounding heath is a central part of the story. Eustacia hates it, while Clym 'might be said to be its product'; it has strong elements that appeal to the primitive in man, as the primitive rites (which have survived Christianity and still persist on the heath) testify – for example those of bonfire night and May Day. There are sections describing the heath in spring in Book 3; in summer in Book 4; and in autumn in Book 5.

To an extent Hardy was describing a countryside that, even as he wrote, was passing away. People still walked wherever they wished, and indeed most people never, in their whole lives, travelled further than they could walk. Time was of no account, and the only clock for most people was the sun.

Villagers' amusements were traditional, connected with age-old country festivals – the bonfire, the mummers' folk-drama at Christmas, the gipsying, the maypole and the serenading of a wedded couple. Honeymoons were quite out of the question, and only the wealthy ever thought of them. Ideas of marriage and society were quite different from those of today, and Wildeve states that what is his wife's is his.

Mrs Yeobright's was typical of the inside of a house, with an 'old-fashioned cavernous fire-place', in which people burned furze or turf. Logs were for special occasions only, and Eustacia is rebuked by Captain Vye for wasting them. In her husband's time Mrs Yeobright sanded the floor of her house. Chimneys were huge, and Wildeve's inn had a large chimney-corner, around which were grouped high-backed settles to keep out any draught. There was no piped water; all water was drawn from wells, and if anything fell down the well it was very difficult to get it up again. The brightest artificial light was lamplight. At the Quiet Woman, the inn brewed its own beer and had not yet been taken over by companies who sold beer of the same brew to all the inns in the district from their own breweries. There were no licensed or unlicensed hours. People kept their money in boxes and did not make use of banks. Village haircuts were hit-or-miss affairs, often done outside the front door in summertime. There was no state education, and Thomasin's maid was a girl of thirteen who did not earn enough to pay for a pair of gloves.

One of the most noticeable differences is that of social class. There is a clear hierarchy on the heath, and Mrs Yeobright considers herself superior to most of the heath-folk, partly because she is a curate's daughter, but also because she has rather more money, and can afford to employ someone of the status of Christian Cantle. This means, too, that she can look down on Eustacia's family, and she has none too high an opinion of Clym's ambition to be a teacher; to see him as a furze-cutter is humiliating. Eustacia's attitude to Charley is condescending, but so is Wildeve's to the rustics who come to the inn. Even he is charitable towards the very poor; he takes a bottle of wine as a present.

Above all, society was thought of as static. It did not enter the consciousness of most people that they might alter their circumstances. The church catechism taught them to stay in the situation to which God had assigned them, and it is a paradox of the novel that Clym Yeobright, the educated man, should want to come back to Egdon. He implicitly accepts this situation, answering his mother's ambitions with 'Mother, what is doing well?'

Chapter summaries, critical commentaries, textual notes and revision questions

Book 1, Chapter 1

One of the most famous of Hardy's set-pieces: a description of Egdon Heath.

Commentary

The Heath is to be the setting for the whole of the novel and its character imposes itself on all the personages who appear in it. For Hardy, one can understand this, as it came right down to his childhood home at Upper Bockhampton, and must have been part of his everyday experience. It is significant that he chooses to start the novel in November. The colours are sombre and the mood threatening – most obviously as regards the weather, where storms and darkness are not far off, but also as Hardy's characterization often fits the mood of the landscape he describes. One can therefore guess that the story is likely to be similarly sombre and that the novel is to be an ill-starred if romantic one.

Darkness and threatening weather in inhospitable country were by the time *The Return of the Native* was written clichés of the Gothic novel and of its romantic successors. What immediately sets *The Return of the Native* apart from the ordinary novel is the closeness of observation it shows (though this is masked to some extent by Hardy's retiring nature), here expressed by a display of learning and literary technique.

The most obvious instance of this in the early paragraphs is in the scholarly vocabulary. Words like 'congruity' and 'champaign' derived from Latin are followed by a series of rhetorical phrases starting with 'majestic without severity'. There is the balance of one phrase against another; the repetition of phrases in 'the façade of a prison ... the façade of a palace'; a good deal of alliteration and assonance. All this is an indication of Hardy's own temperament, which tends to be ascetic, and to be attracted by irony and tragedy rather than by gaiety and triviality. One feels that he prefers Egdon in storm, mist and winter to the same scene in 'summer days of highest feather'. The concluding paragraphs – which sketch the history of the Heath from geological, prehistoric and Roman times through Domesday to the present day – all emphasize how little man has affected the scene. They also imply that this state of affairs is likely to continue.

unenclosed i.e. common land, not yet enclosed through the ownership of any private purchaser.

champaigns Stretches of open country.

approaching its last quarter i.e. it is waning.

The new Vale of Tempe ... Thule The Vale of Tempe is near Mount Olympus in Greece and was famous throughout the classical world for its beauty. Thule was an island at the edge of the known world, reputed to have volcanoes, and today is generally identified with Iceland.

Heidelberg and Baden In Hardy's time fashionable resorts in Germany and Switzerland. He had recently visited them with his wife before he started work on the novel.

Scheveningen A fishing port and holiday resort near The Hague in Holland.

Leland The earliest recorded English antiquary, appointed King's Antiquary by King Henry VIII in 1533.

Ishmaelitish Ishmael was 'a wild man; his hand ... against every man' (Genesis 16.12).

vicinal Neighbouring.

the great Western road of the Romans The road from London to Exeter.

Chapter 2

From out of the setting of Chapter 1 an elderly man walks into the story and catches up with a reddleman walking alongside a cart. The reddleman is uncommunicative, but the old man discovers that there is a woman in the cart. The reddleman forbids him to satisfy his curiosity, says it is no matter who she is, and avoids further questions about her by deciding to rest and leave the old man to go on his way. A woman's form is seen at a distance on a barrow, independent of many other forms who are climbing it, and each depositing a burden at the top.

Commentary

Hardy's main intention in these early chapters is to arouse curiosity, and this one poses a number of mysteries, some of which are resolved only much later. An unimportant character, Cap-

tain Vye, is the first human being to be presented, seen against
the dark background of the Heath. His purpose is to introduce
the first important character, Diggory Venn the reddleman; the
quietness of that introduction gives as yet no hint of the melodrama that is later to surround him. What is strange is Venn's
occupation, and Hardy acknowledges that, even as the story was
being written, that occupation was an anachronism. He firmly
sets the tale about forty years before the year in which *The Return
of the Native* was written.

The reddleman's appearance is described at some length, but
the contents of his van whet the appetite more – indeed Captain
Vye's curiosity, which is blunted by Venn's refusal to tell him
anything, leads the reader into all sorts of suppositions. We
gather that Venn's position is rather like that of the Petrarchan
lover in that the object of his affection is unattainable; when he
so obviously has her in such compromising conditions it
increases our respect for him that he is not one to take advantage of the situation. This adds a degree of pathos, as in any case
Venn's occupation is a lonely one.

As the scene moves to the barrow in the last two pages we are
reminded again of the past before the enigmatic figure of the
girl we are to know as Eustacia climbs to the top, studiously
avoiding those who are building a bonfire on it. We note that
Hardy sees the scene from below, and this serves to magnify the
height of the barrow (not in itself very high) as the land falls
steeply away from it. The scene is described as if in silhouette,
with a curious architectural simile (the dome without the lantern) – and then a significant image as Eustacia disappears ('with
the glide of a water-drop down a bud'). These indicate aspects of
her character – mystery, grace and elegance – which are to be
such a feature of her personality.

boat-cloak A naval officer's cloak.
like the parting-line ... black hair Hardy used the same simile in his
  poem 'The Roman Road'.
Atlantean Belonging to a giant. Atlas was a mythical king charged with
  the responsibility of holding up the sky, and was changed into Mount
  Atlas by Perseus.
Celts Inhabitants of Western Europe in prehistoric times, and later
  forced into its westernmost extremities by pressure of invaders.

Chapter 3

The folk who live in this part of the Heath gather at Rainbarrow, a dominating tumulus, to celebrate by lighting their annual bonfire on the fifth of November, as their ancestors did long before the Gunpowder Plot. There is much conversation as the fire burns, and from it we learn various things relevant to the development of the novel. The most important of these is that, after having stood up in church to forbid the banns of marriage for her niece Thomasin the previous autumn, Mrs Yeobright has now changed her mind and allowed her niece to marry Wildeve, a local publican. The couple have that day gone away to be married at the nearest town, Anglebury. We also learn that her son Clym Yeobright is expected home for Christmas. At the end of the chapter the reddleman comes to the bonfire group to ask the way to Mrs Yeobright's cottage at Blooms-End; as he departs to bring his cart up the rough track, Mrs Yeobright herself appears and talks to the company, while clearly reg⁓⁓d-ing them as not quite in her social class

Commentary

As the fire blazes up the reader feels the intensity of the contrast between the enveloping darkness and the points of light that come from similar bonfires all over the Heath. It is made plain that the custom has continued for many hundreds of years, and it seems a gesture of defiance at the onset of winter. One is therefore led to think of other customs, which may not only antedate Christianity but may be part of a way of life that reflects man's primitive needs. Here the Gunpowder Plot and later Christmas itself seem merely to have been adapted to serve these needs. Hardy's powers of description are here at their best. They reflect his deep sensitivity to atmosphere and are not cluttered by attempts to show his learning.

The rest of the chapter is mostly occupied by a lengthy scene involving the heath-folk. Hardy chooses to use direct speech, with five different characters; he shows that he has an ear for the colourful and the dramatic, and is able to set it down unself-consciously. We are in a world where the scandal of the forbid-den banns proves constant food for conversation, and Hardy's sense of humour is able to emerge through the way Grandfer Cantle, his youngest son Christian, and Susan Nunsuch reveal themselves. The mention of Captain Vye's granddaughter, together with the entry of the reddleman and Mrs Yeobright, serve to collect the characters so far described before the story starts to unfold.

Maenades Female worshippers of Bacchus, Roman god of wine. They were represented with dishevelled hair under an ivy crown, a fawnskin on their shoulders, and a wand wreathed with ivy in their hands.

the sublime Florentine Dante (1265–1321) the greatest Italian poet and author of *The Divine Comedy*. Limbo was an intermediate region between heaven and hell, the abode of the souls of the pious who in their lives had no opportunity to accept Christ (e.g. those who died before his time).

Thor and Woden Old Scandinavian gods: Thor the god of thunder, Woden the chief of the gods.

Druidical The Druids were priests of the ancient Celts.

Gunpowder Plot A plot when Guy Fawkes attempted to blow up Parliament, 5 November 1605; since commemorated in England by bonfires and fireworks.

the winter ingress The onset of winter.

Promethean In classical mythology, Prometheus stole fire from the gods and brought it to earth for the use of man.

Düreresque In the style of Dürer, a German painter (1471–1528).

The king call'd down ... may be From a ballad in Percy's *Reliques* called 'Queen Eleanor's confession'.

stave Song.

weasand Throat.

forbad the banns Before a wedding the custom is that notice be read out in church three times, and any objectors to the marriage be invited to state their objections. At the time of the novel weddings were not allowed anywhere other than in church.

the Philistine's greaves of brass i.e those of Goliath (1 Samuel 17.6).

tide-times Regular festivals e.g. Christmas-tide, Eastertide.

in the year four i.e. 1804. The old man is proud of his being asked to help defend England against Napoleon.

thy father's cross People who cannot write are allowed to make a cross instead of writing a signature.

dog days The time when the dogstar Sirius rises with the sun (3 July– 11 August) and the hottest time of the year.

tear her smock i.e. do rough work.

maphrotight A corruption of 'hermaphrodite' – an abnormal person (or animal) with characteristics of both sexes.

no moon, no man A very old country superstition referred to by Shakespeare (The Tempest II, 2, 115).

The Great Book of the Judgment Here, the register of baptisms.

Lammas-tide The festival of the first-fruits of corn, 1 August.

ballet A song.

skinful i.e. of liquor.
kex The stem of any reed or plant when hollowed out and the pith extracted.
well-favoured Good-looking.
pattens Overshoes; wooden-soled shoes with rings or bars of iron under the wood to keep them out of the mud.
poussetted Waltzed.
vlankers Capers.
death's head Skull.
Nebo The mountain from which Moses was to view the Land of Canaan – the promised land which he was never to enjoy (Deuteronomy 32 48–52).

Chapter 4

The girl in the reddleman's van was Thomasin. Her aunt meets the reddleman near the inn owned by Damon Wildeve, Thomasin's intended husband; she discovers that Thomasin has come back home unmarried and walks home with her.

Commentary

Little that we do not know already is added to the story here, apart from the circumstances of Thomasin's arrival in the reddleman's van. Mrs Yeobright is confirmed as decisive, Venn as retiring and discreet, Thomasin as a timorous maiden in distress; and the reader's curiosity moves somewhat nearer satisfaction.

Tartarean Belonging to the infernal regions (Tartarus in Latin).
what's done cannot be undone Lady Macbeth's words (*Macbeth*, V,1,74).
Amerigo Vespucci The Italian who gave his name to the newly discovered continent of America.
what's the meaning ... performance Intended to whet the reader's appetite for the next episode; like most Victorian novels, this one was serialized in a periodical.

Chapter 5

As soon as they are out of earshot of the reddleman, Mrs Yeobright's manner towards her niece changes. Thomasin says that she was not married 'because of some trifling irregularity in the licence'. Her aunt takes her to the Quiet Woman for an explanation from Wildeve, and discovers that the licence was made out for a wedding in Budmouth and not in Anglebury. Wildeve tells Thomasin that they will be married on Monday (it is Saturday night).

Just then the heath-people come to congratulate the newly wedded couple and to drink their health – in mead provided by the host – not knowing that under the circumstances their attentions are far from welcome. When Wildeve goes back to the room where he had left aunt and niece, they have both gone.

Wildeve goes out to leave a bottle of wine at the cottage of a heath-dweller. All the evening he has been aware of a bonfire, which seems to have been lit as a signal, and on leaving the cottage he presses on rapidly along a path that leads under Rainbarrow towards the beckoning light.

Commentary

The explanation of Thomasin's mishap can only be seen as an anticlimax; when it has been so long delayed, a mere irregularity over the licence is one of several disappointments over events early in the novel, which seem to be moving to a climax that never comes. It means too that Wildeve, as one of the more important characters, is first presented in a curiously unimpressive way, especially when he is measured against the redoubtable Mrs Yeobright. The rustic chorus arriving to serenade what they think is the newly married couple are as much a contrast here as they were two chapters before – blissfully unaware of how inappropriate their visit is as they enliven what would otherwise be a melancholy atmosphere. One notes the ludicrous contrast between the 'strong bass' and the 'wheezy thin piping' of Grandfer and Christian Cantle and the respect amounting almost to reverence that they show towards the dead Mr Yeobright before they depart.

Wildeve appears early as a womanizer. To go moth-like towards Eustacia's beacon on the day he should have married Thomasin reinforces the casualness he has displayed earlier, and cannot promise well for their marriage when – and at this stage one has almost to say if – it takes place.

Gothic With a pointed arch.
Whenever a club walked *Tess of the D'Urbervilles* opens with a village

club-walking, the relics of a May Day dance – whose 'singularity lay less in the retention of a custom of walking in procession and dancing on each anniversary than in the members being solely women'. The description of Mr Yeobright is a reminder of the time when music in church was provided not by an organ, but by a local band sitting on a gallery. Hardy's father was a regular member of such a band.

to 'Lydia' All hymn tunes have names and this is the one sung to Psalm 133 in a metrical version.

as if he'd been in no common clothes Cf. 'turning all at once into a common man no holier than you or I' (Chapter 3).

Farinelli's singing ... Begum speech Famous occasions in the life of each. Farinelli was the professional name of Carlo Broschi (1705–82) who became Court singer to King Philip V of Spain. Sheridan's 'Begum' speech was on the impeachment of Warren Hastings, Governor-General of India (1787), which Pitt said 'surpassed all the eloquence of ancient and modern times'. It concerned the seizing by Warren Hastings of part of the treasure of the mother and the grandmother of the late Vizier of Oude (the Begums) under false charges. It lasted from 6.30 p.m. until midnight on 7 February 1787.

when a woman deliberates ... she is lost (Addison's *Cato* 4,1,31).

Chapter 6

The first figure on Rainbarrow (see end of Chapter 2) is there again, and apparently despondent. She descends to the small undying bonfire outside Captain Vye's house. She had lit the fire as a signal for Wildeve to come, as she did on the same day twelve months before.

Her grandfather had told her of a broken-off wedding and she thought that Wildeve had not married Thomasin because he had been faithful to her. Wildeve arrives in response to her summons. He is cool towards her but still finds her attractive. Her feeling for him is much more passionate.

Commentary

There is a strong poetic element in *The Return of the Native* and nowhere is this more evident than in the early section of this chapter. The woman on the Barrow is mysterious and her mystery has not entirely disappeared by the end. Hardy's description of the wind blowing over the Heath has the power of deep feeling combined with intimate knowledge that can be spoken of most effectively in metaphorical terms – as a communion or a consummation.

We have first seen Eustacia Vye as a silhouette, and here in the darkness her spectral appearance is only gradually brought down to earth; we see her by the light of a live coal, then by that of the bonfire itself. Her walking down scarcely-known paths and her behaviour towards Johnny Nunsuch and her grandfather further confirm her aloofness and reserve. But the climax is reached as Wildeve arrives in answer to her summons. Eustacia's morality is seen to be primitive: she wishes to assert her power, to defeat Thomasin, the girl she can only see as a wholly inadequate rival, and to win control over any male with whom she may come into contact – while giving away nothing herself. This refinement of selfishness matches the extreme atmosphere that Hardy has created.

Homer's Cimmerian land A mythical land in the farthest West, enveloped in mist and darkness.
fetichistic A favourite word of Hardy's – acting like a spell or charm.
Sappho and Mrs Siddons The first was an ancient Greek poetess, traditionally (though not historically) immoral, and the second was the greatest tragic actress in England at the beginning of the nineteenth century.
members i.e. limbs.
like that which troubled Belshazzar Which wrote mysteriously on the wall at Belshazzar's Feast (Daniel 5).
parian A fine white porcelain resembling Parian marble (see also note p.42).
Albertus Magnus A European scholar of the mid-thirteenth century.
Hypochondriasis Morbid depression – especially about one's health.
as the Witch ... Samuel see 1 Samuel 28, 3–20.

Chapter 7

A description of Eustacia Vye.

Commentary

The description of Eustacia reveals what the visual images we have had so far could not: her ancestry, and the reasons behind her situation. The closeness of the description on the first two pages suggests that the portrait is based upon an actual person, and a series of comparisons in which Hardy shows the breadth of his knowledge cannot completely conceal the fact that Eustacia's nature is dominated in everything she does by the great Victorian unmentionable – sexual passion. The blaze of the bonfire can thus clearly be seen in two senses, symbolic as well as literal; her impatience with the Heath and with the conventions of its inhabitants show that she has inherited the restless sexuality of her father, together with something of his artistic temperament. In this strength of imagination she is very much part of the romantic core of the novel.

Olympus A mountain in Macedonia, supposed by the ancients to be the abode of the gods.

the distaff ... the shears The emblems of the Fates, three sisters in classical mythology, representing birth, life and death.

like the Sphinx i.e. imponderable, enigmatic.

Ulex Europaeus The Latin name for the furze bush.

cima-recta or ogee An architectural term for a moulding forming an S-shape.

of an arch Introduced about 1300 and in the shape of an upper lip.

forgotten marbles Broken statues.

Sleswig South of Denmark, between the North Sea and the Baltic.

Bourbon i.e. royal, beautiful. Bourbon was the name of the French royal family before 1789.

lotus-eaters ... 'Athalie' i.e. opposite moods. The lotus plant, according to Homer, produced a state of languor, whereas the march in 'Athalie' is a stirring march by Mendelssohn (1843).

Artemis, Athena or Hera respectively (1) was the goddess of hunting and of chastity, (2) the goddess of war and wisdom and the liberal arts, similarly impervious to the passion of love, (3) the queen of the gods, an exacting and jealous wife. They are often known by their Roman names: Diana, Minerva and Juno.

Tartarean Belonging to the infernal regions.

Richter A German writer (1763–1825).

Corfiote A native of Corfu, one of the Ionian islands, between Greece and Italy.

Alcinous' line Homer represents him as the happy ruler of the Phaecians (his name for the inhabitants of Corfu).

Fitzalan and De Vere Names typical of the English peerage.

'a populous solitude' The figure of speech known as oxymoron, where words of opposite meaning are placed together, making an apparent contradiction. (Here Byron's *Childe Harold*, 3,1,101.)

told Counted.

Strafford The Earl of Strafford (1593–1641) was sent by Charles I to Ireland as Lord Deputy in 1631. There he was given the nickname 'Thorough', and was ultimately impeached and executed.

Saul or Sisera i.e. those who had fought hard against great odds. Sisera was the captain of the host of Hazor into whose hand the Lord sold the Israelites when they had forgotten him (Judges 4,2; 1 Samuel 12,9).

Ultimately he was slain by a woman (Judges, 5, 25–31). Eustacia admired them more than the conventional biblical heroes, Jacob and David.

oracles of Delphian ambiguity The oracle at Delphi gave prophecies that could be interpreted in a number of ways.

between the Héloïses and the Cleopatras Héloïse (1101–64), the daughter of Canon Fulbert of Notre Dame, was famous for her romantic love for Cleopatra was the famous Egyptian queen whose beauty overcame first Julius Caesar and then Mark Antony. They stand here for noble and base love, and in heaven Eustacia will probably sit between the two.

Chapter 8

The reddleman helps the boy who had kept up Eustacia's bonfire when he has a fall and cuts his hand; he learns that she had met a gentleman there, and guesses that Wildeve is playing a devious game.

Commentary

The function of Chapter 8 is to inform Venn of the meeting between Eustacia and Wildeve, the starting-point of many of the events of the novel. He is thereby given the occasion to protect his beloved Thomasin. Hardy's scenes are highly visual; here the darkness increases the effect of the vivid red that permeates Venn as he is spotlit by the stove inside his van. The fact that the image of the reddleman was used to frighten children is the main reason why Johnny Nunsuch is initially frightened of him. But all Venn's attempts to explain this rationally do not completely conceal the fact that there is just a hint of the supernatural about him, something the rest of the novel develops.

Scyllaeo-Charybdean Scylla was a dangerous rock in the strait between Sicily and the mainland of Italy. In sailing through it, sailors attempted to avoid it, and were often sucked into a whirlpool on the opposite side (Charybdis).

clog A metal device attached to a horse's foot.

tilt A cover for a wagon, usually of canvas.

Chapter 9

The reddleman waits for a week after their meeting, overheard by the boy in the previous chapter, before Eustacia and Wildeve meet again. He overhears the moody talk of two people who in spite of bursts of anger and uncertainty seem unable to resist each other. He decides to see Eustacia.

Commentary

The lengthy description of the reddleman and his habits is a reminder that, at the time Hardy wrote the novel, reddlemen were things of the past. He set *The Return of the Native* about 1840, the date of his own birth, but solitariness seems to be the only characteristic of reddlemen much used in the character of Venn after his arresting introduction. The letter written by Venn to Thomasin two years previously indicates that his feeling for her is something of an obsession – in this novel of characters with obsessions.

His attempts to witness Wildeve's and Eustacia's meeting shows the novelist writing with a new technique. Up to now he has been the omniscient writer, knowing his characters' innermost thoughts; now Hardy shares this with Venn, the first instance of many in which apparently private conversations are overheard by someone else. In the process Wildeve is revealed as a somewhat passionless philanderer, while Eustacia's longing for a passion that will sweep her away is muted after the previous chapter.

Mephistophelian Like the devil – because are red. Mephistopheles first appears in the German *Faustbuch* (16th century) as a helper of the devil.
Arab i.e. nomad.
as with the mark of Cain Which God put on him when he had murdered his brother Abel (Genesis 4,15).
becall me Call me names.
the one ewe-lamb ... to him As that in Nathan's parable to David (2 Samuel 12, 1–7).
Tantalus In classical mythology, punished with a raging thirst while water flowed all round him; it always receded when he tried to drink.
Wisconsin A mid-west state in the USA.

Chapter 10

Next morning Venn pleads with Eustacia to give up Wildeve, but she refuses point-blank.

Commentary

Venn's behaviour here can only be called naive. Eustacia is able to make the most of her situation and does so with instinctive self-confidence. In her purposeful delaying to see him, her casual manner and dignified scorn towards all his proposals, she is reacting in a way that has a large emotional and minute logical content. All the time she appears inscrutable and it is only the omniscient author who tells what she feels; Venn allows his emotions to appear in his expression. The chapter ends with all his efforts having succeeded mainly in stimulating her interest in Wildeve; but at least it does make him reconsider his tactics.

In the course of the chapter we have been informed of Egdon's bird life and the reader will remember the portrait of the Heath's hills appearing like islands in a sea of mist.

Aegean That part of the Mediterranean sea between Greece and Asia Minor, thickly studded with small islands.

bustard A marsh bird, now a rare visitor to Britain, which last bred in this country early in the nineteenth century.

Marsh harriers Another rare bird of prey which nests in marshy land.

courser A swift-running bird – a rare visitor from North Africa.

Polaris The pole-star.

Franklin Sir John Franklin (1786–1847), a famous Arctic explorer whose final expedition ended disastrously.

Frederick . . . Queen of Prussia Frederick the Great of Prussia made war on the Archduchess of Austria, Maria Theresa, in 1740; Napoleon on Louisa, Queen of Prussia in the Battle of Jena, 1806. In each of these wars, the victor was the male monarch.

cotters Cottagers.

tiger-beetle An insect of variegated colour, swift and active in movement and preying upon other insects.

withywind Bindweed or convolvulus.

hauteur Haughtiness (Fr.).

the mortification of Candaules' wife Candaules, King of Lydia in Greek mythology, boasted of his wife's beauty and affronted her by allowing her to be seen unveiled by Gyges. In her anger she persuaded Gyges to murder her husband, then married him. He then became King of Lydia.

a Carthaginian . . . and beauty According to tradition Carthage was founded by Dido and soon became a powerful and flourishing city. Tarentum was an important Greek city in Italy, and Baiae, near Naples, was the favourite watering-place of the Romans.

Zenobia Queen of Palmyra, an ancient city in an oasis of the great Syrian desert, who, when she tried to extend her kingdom, came into conflict with Rome.

Chapter 11

The reddleman meets Mrs Yeobright on her way to see Wildeve so that Thomasin can appear before the world with an unblemished character. He reveals to her his former proposal to Thomasin and makes another one to her now, thereby unwittingly putting into her hands a weapon for her interview with Wildeve. At that interview Wildeve gives no direct answer and promises to let her know his decision in a day or two.

Her visit sends Wildeve to Eustacia after dark. He wants to marry her and escape overseas to America. But now that he is no longer coveted by her rival, Eustacia's interest in him wanes perceptibly, and she in her turn promises him an answer by Monday week at the Rainbarrow. She hears from her grandfather that Clym Yeobright is coming home from Paris to spend Christmas with his mother.

Commentary

There is further indication here of Eustacia's need to dominate, and to attract Wildeve's ardour. As soon as she realizes that she has succeeded, we can see her changing as she struggles constantly for the unattainable. Hardy chooses to convey this in dialogue that has both Eustacia and Wildeve talking in a standard English, in noticeable contrast to the language used by the heath-dwellers. Although Hardy hints at a wider, more experienced background for them both in Eustacia's parents and Wildeve's engineering experience, the differentiation is rather improbable.

By the end of the first 'Book' of the novel, the identities of the three women of the title have become clear. Their personalities are clearly contrasted. With the advent of Clym the structure of the novel starts to become clearer as three men now compete for the attentions of two women.

Cellaret Cabinet containing small bottles.

Revision questions on Book 1

1 How far has Hardy succeeded in making Egdon Heath a direct influence on the characters in his novel?

2 What use does Hardy make of darkness in this first part?

3 Contrast the characters of Thomasin and Eustacia as they have emerged so far.

4 What use has Hardy made of the Chorus of Rustics in the first part?

5 'The scenes are constantly melodramatic.' Do you agree?

6 'Wildeve and Venn are both insipid characters.' Is this true?

Book 2, Chapter 1

Eustacia overhears a conversation in which two rustics link her name with that of Clym Yeobright. She takes a walk to Mrs Yeobright's house.

Commentary

The overheard conversation – that favourite device of Hardy's – is used again to tell Eustacia of Clym's arrival. She hears it from two of the rustics, and the interesting feature of their conversation is that they share Captain Vye's view of Paris as a focus of deadly sin. No character in this novel takes any other point of view, with the exception of Eustacia. For the heath-folk that would be understandable; several of them think of her as a witch. Their thoughts of matching her with the new arrival would certainly have had the opposite effect had they been made directly to her. As it is she has a new challenge.

the *Triumph* Hardy's name for Nelson's *Victory*.
to Jericho A familiar Bible name, often colloquially used for a place that is out of the way (founded on the story in 2 Samuel 10, 4–5).
the Castle of Indolence A poem by James Thomson (1700–48). The wizard Indolence ('the invading bard') sings his prelude in Canto 1 stanzas 9–19, the effect of which is (stanza 22) that, '. . . soon as touched by his unhallowed paw,/They found themselves within the cursed gate,/Full hard to be repassed, like that of Fate.'

Chapter 2

Inside Mrs Yeobright's house, Thomasin and her aunt are making preparations for Christmas and for Clym's return; they then go to gather holly on the Heath. We learn that Clym once loved Thomasin.

Commentary

We see the preparations for the coming festivities through the eyes of his mother and cousin. The scene is expressed largely in dialogue that has the effect of sharpening both characters. Two of the episodes are particularly vivid: Thomasin taking apples from the loft and removing the covering bracken as the sunlight catches her hair, and the cutting of the holly where the contrasting scarlet of the berries and the dark green of the foliage are made to stand out strongly by the winter sunshine.

Chapter 3

Just within the Heath Eustacia hears a 'good night' from Clym, who happens to pass by with two women. That night she has a vivid dream, and as she wakes, cries 'O that I had seen his face!' She is half in love with a vision. She wanders towards parts of the Heath with a view towards Blooms-End every day for a week, but does not see him once, and resolves to look no more.

Commentary

For Clym's actual arrival the point of view changes back to Eustacia, and again her first near-meeting with him takes place in darkness. Her romantic nature starts to weave fantasies around the visitor from Paris and reaches a climax in her dream. Fanciful this may be but it is also prophetic and has a strong measure of irony, from the knight in shining armour whose image is suddenly shattered to the intrusion of pools on the Heath. Eustacia's frenzied journeys to gaze towards Blooms-End show that there is much of the adolescent about her, despite her apparent sophistication.

The deaf Dr Kitto A biblical scholar (1804–1854) who was struck stone-deaf through a fall at the age of twelve. The description to which Hardy refers is in his book *The Lost Senses – Deafness and Blindness* (1845).

from Nebuchadnezzar to the Swaffham tinker i.e. from the King of Babylon to a common pedlar today. Daniel told Nebuchadnezzar what

his dream was (Daniel, 2). The Swaffham pedlar is a figure in Norfolk folklore.
the Cretan labyrinth Where the monster Minotaur lived.
Northern Lights The Aurora borealis.
parterre A patterned arrangement of flower-beds.
Queen Scheherazade The daughter of the vizier of King Shahriyar, who married the King and escaped death (the usual fate of his wives) only by telling him the stories in *The Arabian Nights*.
perfervid Very ardent.
circumambulated Walked around.

Chapter 4

One of the Egdon mummers calls to ask permission of Eustacia to use her grandfather's fuel-house as a place to rehearse their parts. The first night's performance is to be at a party at Mrs Yeobright's, and Eustacia wins over the boy to let her take his part – that of the Turkish Knight.

Commentary

Hardy writes of the Christmas mummers' play with a gentle and slightly patronizing humour, though he felt a deep affection for it as an example of a way of life that had continued since time immemorial. Eustacia, we are told, feels contempt for its crudity, but is ready to forget her objection if it gives her the opportunity to see the new arrival. Her scheme shows energy, originality, self-confidence and a measure of deviousness. Her treatment of Charley is not without some pathos, and is a good example of Hardy's sense of humour at work. The intensity of Charley's feelings while holding her hand is a measure of the awe in which the heath-dwellers hold this girl who is so unlike them.

A Tussaud collection i.e. like those at Madame Tussaud's, a famous exhibition of waxwork figures in London.
like Baalam The prophet, who only half-heartedly cursed Israel for the King of Moab, and ultimately prophesied that Israel would do valiantly (Numbers, 22–24).
the well-known play of St George Hardy was familiar with this play which he had seen at village festivals, and he was one of those who assisted in restoring the text of the play when it was published in 1928.
basinet A light globular headpiece.

a Raffaelle after Perugino Raffaelle or Raphael (1483–1520) studied under Perugino and first cleverly imitated his style, then outclassed him.

fire-dog Iron bars, which support logs in a wood fire.

Chapter 5

Eustacia plays her part in Mrs Yeobright's house, but has little leisure for observation.

Commentary

The main interest here lies in the close description of the Christmas festivities at Blooms-End at a time when all entertainments had to be home-made. It is important of course that Eustacia should be there, but what she does is perhaps less important than the atmosphere that Hardy evokes: the contrast between the anticipation of the mummers as they walk over a frosty heath to a picture-book thatched cottage and the warmth, activity and noise of the interior lit by candles and the peat fire. The Father Christmas with a club has nothing in common with today's white-bearded and red-coated version, but a great deal with a medieval fertility figure; and the extraordinary appeal of the scene owes everything to the fact that it recreates an idealized past and invites comparison with what was becoming, as Hardy wrote the novel, a steadily more commercialized present.

the serpent An old bass musical instrument. It has a tapered leather-covered tube eight feet long, twisted like a serpent.

pyracanth An evergreen shrub, often grown against a wall, noted for its orange berries in the autumn and for its vicious thorns.

Chapter 6

Eustacia has an opportunity to look closely at Clement Yeobright as she lies 'dead' against the clock-case, and there is a full description of him. The mummers stay to have supper. Then Eustacia slips outside, followed by Clym; he asks her if she is a woman, but neither reveals her secret nor asks awkward questions.

Outside the wicket-gate at home she remembers that she had promised to meet Wildeve that night at eight, and regrets that she had been the main cause of the postponement of his marriage to Thomasin.

Commentary

This chapter moves much more slowly than its predecessor. The description of Clym starts from Eustacia's point of view, but the omniscient author soon takes over and reflects in leisurely and learned fashion over his appearance; Eustacia's attitude is more feverish than leisurely. A contrasting episode of rustic humour gives a stir to the action before the austere Eustacia slips outside. Her first meeting with Clym is as melodramatic as all her appearances have been, and her striding alone across the lonely Heath by moonlight in her costume maintains this aura to the last paragraph.

an Etna of peat i.e. smoking like a volcano.

in Rembrandt's intensest manner Rembrandt (1606–69) was the greatest painter of the Dutch school; he specialized in searching portraits with a dark background.

Jared, Mahalaleel According to Genesis 5, 20 and 17, they lived for 962 and 895 years respectively.

the coil of things A favourite phrase of Hardy's, which well expresses the fatalism of his outlook.

the second Lord Lyttleton His death-warning dream is said to have occasioned his death, which took place in 1779.

When the disguised Queen of Love . . . her quality When Venus appeared before her son (Aeneas), as told in Virgil's *Aeneid*.

the doom of Echo To speak only in repetition of someone else. She fell desperately in love with Narcissus, but as her love was not returned she pined away in grief and became a lingering voice.

Polly Peachum A character in Gay's *Beggar's Opera*. The Miss Fentom who played her became the Duchess of Bolton. Lydia Languish is a character in Sheridan's *The Rivals*. Miss Harriott Mellon played her in a revival of the play, and for her second husband (in 1827) married the Duke of St Albans.

perfervid Very ardent.

Chapter 7

Eustacia comes across Venn's caravan in a hollow of the heath. She suggests that he is to marry Thomasin, and embarrasses him. Just then she sees Wildeve approaching and, wishing to avoid him, asks for refuge inside Venn's caravan. Venn guesses that her feeling for Wildeve has changed; she confirms this, and the reddleman offers to carry a letter for her with the presents that Wildeve had given her. Wildeve resolves to marry Thomasin partly to spite Eustacia, goes to claim her at Blooms-End, and gets her just before Venn arrives. Venn is spoken to by Mrs Yeobright and departs empty-handed.

Commentary

As the competition for the two women moves towards its resolution the reader is led to compare the naked self-interest that motivates Eustacia and Wildeve with the altruism of Venn. The material is presented with the humorous parallels between Venn's offering to Wildeve of unpalatable information, and a little later Wildeve's getting his own back in identical terms.

Ahasuerus the Jew Presumably the King of Persia of the Book of Esther, called here the Jew in reference to his pro-Jewish policy after he divorced Vashti and was married to Esther, whose cousin Mordecai the Jew (who brought her up) he advanced. The Book of Esther illustrates his restlessness.

in Zin In the wilderness (Numbers 22, 1–5).

This Ishmaelitish creature i.e. wild (Genesis 16, 12).

pis aller (Fr.) Used for want of anything better.

like Satan . . . Ithuriel's spear When he had been found in Paradise in the disguise of a toad and started up 'discovered and surpriz'd' (*Paradise Lost*, 4, 813).

resolve to marry in haste A typical piece of Hardy irony. Though it is not stated here, the English proverb is 'Marry in haste and repent at leisure.'

Chapter 8

Thomasin – familiarly known as Tamsin – marries Wildeve. In the absence of anyone else, Eustacia gives her away and signs the register with 'sincerest pleasure'. Venn disappears from the area for several months.

Commentary

Hardy's instinct is to dramatize a situation wherever possible, and here the whole of Mrs Yeobright's discussion with Tamsin is expressed in direct speech. The wedding preparations are somewhat melancholy, and only the braiding of Tamsin's hair and her blue dress seen against the brown of the Heath enliven the scene.

The wedding itself is muted by being in reported speech, and because it was arranged to take place during Clym's absence. The presence of Eustacia and her giving the bride away revive the hint of melodrama that has continually attended her, and what should have been a happy occasion ends the second section of the book in a minor key.

Revision questions on Book 2

1 How are the following characters developed in this section: Eustacia, Venn, Thomasin?

2 How is the interest built up before Clym's arrival, and how is it sustained after it?

3 What part does the Heath play in this section?

4 Assess the importance of local customs and how well they are integrated into the development of the novel.

5 How far does Hardy dramatize important scenes in the first two sections?

Book 3, Chapter 1

Clym stays at home long after local gossip expects him to have returned to Paris at the end of the holiday. He tells a group waiting for a haircut that he is dissatisfied with Paris, intends to stay and start a school close to Egdon, and is going to study for the necessary qualifications.

Commentary

Clym Yeobright is the portrait of the local lad who has made good, and who as a result excites great curiosity among the heath-folk. The description is a leisurely one, with several refer-ences to the classics as parallels for his appearance and tempera-ment; and in the novel it cannot be coincidence that the only other character afforded this generosity of treatment is Eustacia. The rustic chorus lightens the tone with the performance of the ritual haircut, but Clym's entrance immediately expresses his moral earnestness and extinguishes the spark they had kindled. His negligible sense of humour can in the circumstances only be called ominous.

'My mind to me a kingdom is' The first line of the best-known poem of Sir Edward Dyer (c. 1550–1607).
Pheidias The greatest sculptor of ancient Greece (c. 490–432 BC), and supposedly responsible for the Parthenon sculptures (the Elgin Marbles).
Aeschylus Greek dramatist (525–456 BC).
Gracian A Jesuit and man of letters, rector of the Jesuit college at Tarragona, north-east Spain (1584–1658).
with tiger-lily pollen . . . in the absence of water-colours Such painting materials were commonly used by poor village boys in the first half of the nineteenth century.
like Homer's i.e. the time and place of his birth are unknown.
Clive . . . Keats All these men became famous in fields other than those in which they had begun. Clive became famous as the founder of the British Indian Empire, Gay as the author of *The Beggar's Opera* and Keats as a poet.
dinner-time i.e. midday.

Chapter 2

Clym tells his mother that he is not going back to Paris, but feels he has a mission to spread education to the people of Egdon Heath. To his mother this is a waste of his talents, and she is clearly unhappy about it. Christian Cantle then calls at Blooms-End with news that Eustacia has been jabbed with a stocking needle in church by Susan Nunsuch; in drawing blood she has sought to stop Eustacia's supposed witchcraft. Clym is interested in her; he seeks an opportunity to find out more about her and to go to Mistover.

Commentary

The hints of the previous chapter are enlarged, and Hardy acknowledges that Clym has something of the zealot in his makeup as he proclaims his affection for the Heath and his mission to educate it. For the first time this brings out the potential for conflict between him and his mother, whose ambitions lie in a more worldly direction. These are most potently summarized in his question, 'Mother, what is doing well?'

The arrival of Christian Cantle pursues the pattern of the previous chapter, where rustic humour is introduced to lighten a chapter threatening to become too serious; but here its purpose is altogether different, to report the attack on Eustacia. While this is a development of what the heath-folk have earlier said about her, it has the same tinge of melodrama that she carries wherever she goes. In particular it seems to be focused on the church, which has earlier been the scene for the forbidding of Tamsin's banns, not to mention her clandestine wedding. All three of these incidents are reported and are thus distanced from the main narrative. The attack on Eustacia, however, emphasizes the primitive rhythms that dominate Egdon. Clym's interest in Eustacia carries clear potential for conflict – between Clym's belief in his evangelizing power, his mother's uncompromising and restless ambition for him, and Eustacia's obsessive desire to leave the Heath.

a John the Baptist . . . for his text John the Baptist called upon men to repent: 'Repent ye: for the kingdom of heaven is at hand (Matthew 3,2).

Philip's warlike son Alexander the Great, the son of Philip of Macedon.

ancient Chaldeans The wise men of Babylon (See Daniel 2).

the poetry of Rogers . . . the spiritual guidance of Sumner These references were much more topical when the novel was published in 1878 than they are now. Samuel Rogers (1763–1855) wrote mediocre poetry as a hobby (but not as a living – he was a banker). Benjamin West (1738–1820) was a skilful but uninspired painter. Lord North (1733–92), a weak minister 1770–82, was responsible for the loss of the American colonies. John Bird Sumner (1780–1862) was an undistinguished Archbishop of Canterbury from 1848.

plashed With their branches bound down and interweaved.

as St Paul says Romans 8,22.

Plato's Socrates His *Apology* for or defence of Socrates, his old teacher, whose philosophy he developed.

Pontius Pilate See John 18,38.

Chapter 3

Mrs Yeobright regretfully sees her son's growing yearning for Eustacia. He goes to help in getting Captain Vye's bucket up from the bottom of the well and Eustacia's concern for him is suddenly evident. Clym gets into conversation with her, and in attempting to obtain a bucket of fresh water she hurts her hand. In the following conversation she makes it plain that she finds the Heath uncongenial, while he says how much he loves it. She is unenthusiastic about his plan to educate the heath-folk, but Clym scarcely notices this in his enthusiasm.

A barrow on the heath is opened, and on second thoughts Clym gives a pot of the bones to Eustacia, instead of to his mother; mother and son quarrel.

Commentary

Nearly three months pass by in the course of this chapter. The recovery of the lost bucket, the main occasion where the growing friendship develops, is beautifully written, and shows the Egdon community actively helping one another, stylistically making an interesting contrast to what has gone before yet at the same time blending with it. The meeting of the two lovers-to-be, while not accidental, is made to seem so. Mrs Yeobright's opposition to the developing affair is totally instinctive – partly the feeling of many mothers that no woman is good enough for her son, and partly a rationalization of dislike for a person she believes is leading a purposeless existence. In Eustacia she can see only pride and conceit; a situation loaded with irony, as she seems totally unaware that these sins are not entirely absent from her own personality. As ever, Hardy chooses to convey this by dialogue, and Clym's speeches show a man sublimely self-confident that Eustacia will be ready to cooperate with his plans, ignoring the fact that her obsession is running in a contrary direction.

One notices the symbolism of the ashes of the fire which once summoned Wildeve; of the well; and of the resurrection of nature from the pond.

Parian marble A marble from The Greek island of Paros. See also note on 'parian', p.27).
Blacklock Thomas Blacklock DD (1721–91), called 'the blind poet', lost his sight through smallpox before he was six months old.
Professor Sanderson Nicholas Sanderson (1682–1739) also lost his sight through smallpox when he was only one year old, yet became a Fellow of the Royal Society.
Sallaert, Van Alsloot Two little-known Flemish painters of the early seventeenth and late sixteenth centuries respectively. Hardy was very

interested in art and had seen their work on a continental tour two
years before he wrote *The Return of the Native*.

Chapter 4

Clym goes out to see Eustacia on Rainbarrow, though he tells his
mother that it is to see an eclipse of the moon. The lovers'
infatuation with each other is increasing, but they have little in
common mentally; in his calmer moments Clym recognizes this.

Commentary

The setting for the climactic love-meeting where Clym and
Eustacia have the author as a commentator on their tryst keeps
up the melodramatic flavour of the novel, for it takes place at
Rainbarrow during a lunar eclipse – not something that happens
every day of the week. The lovers as well as the reader can see
the symbolic aspect of this; the reader is aware too of the earlier
occasion when Wildeve stood in Clym's place. Both Clym and
Eustacia are constantly aware of issues that might obstruct their
love, but equally ready to forget them in the intoxication of
physical attraction, and in the hope that the troublesome issues
will miraculously disappear.

At the end of the chapter we see a more realistic Clym, but
even here, one who is totally unwilling to compromise.

the Tuileries and the Louvre The Tuileries are gardens stretching
 from the Place de la Concorde towards the Louvre (formerly a palace
 and now a picture gallery and museum).
Versailles The former palace of the Kings of France, eleven miles
 south-west of Paris, with extensive grounds that are the setting for
 smaller royal residences, the Trianons. The Little Trianon has
 particular appeal for an Englishman, as it was built for the doomed
 Louis XVI and his queen Marie Antoinette, and near it lies Le jardin
 anglais, built to imitate English landscape gardening. Eustacia's dislike
 of anything English – which she considers provincial – and love of the
 exotic is expressed by the names Fontainebleau, St Cloud, the Bois.
Olympian i.e. like a goddess (who lived on Mount Olympus).
Petrarch for his Laura Petrarch, an Italian poet (1304–74) is famous
 for his odes and sonnets to Laura, the wife of a local Count – hence the
 reference to his chaste love.

Chapter 5

Clym admits his engagement when challenged by his mother, and after a quarrel he decides to leave home on the very day when he had hoped to arrange a meeting between Mrs Yeobright and Eustacia. He meets Eustacia alone; they decide to get married in a fortnight, to live in a tiny cottage for about six months, and then take a house in Budmouth – if no misfortune intervenes.

Commentary

Mrs Yeobright's opposition to the marriage is comprehensive and instinctive, and in just two pages the breach between the mother and son is close to being unbridgable. In contrast the spring weather is used to symbolize the growing affection between Clym and Eustacia; the hollow where they meet with its luxuriant vegetation and 'vaporous warmth' has a quality most unlike that of the heath, and carries clear suggestions of physical passion as they fix the date of their marriage.

no bird sang A clear echo of Keats's poem *La Belle Dame Sans Merci*, which has the line 'And no birds sing'. There too a young man is bewitched by a lady who comes from the supernatural.
Carpe diem (Latin. Horace, *Odes*, 11,7) Pick the fruits of the day, i.e. enjoy an experience and do not think of the future.
cut the knot i.e. swept all difficulties out of the way. In Greek mythology an oracle declared that whoever could untie a complex knot, tied by Gordius, King of Phrygia, would rule the world. Alexander the Great solved the problem by cutting the knot with his sword.
both being of full age A slight inconsistency. Hardy has earlier said that Eustacia was only nineteen (2,1) – not 21.

Chapter 6

Clym leaves home. There is a barrier between him and his mother. Early the same afternoon Tamsin comes to see her aunt. Among other things, she says that Wildeve keeps her short of money, and Mrs Yeobright reminds her that she has some money to be divided between her and Clym.

Wildeve's old longing for Eustacia returns when he discovers that she is about to be married to Clym.

Commentary

It is characteristic of Clym, as of his mother, to proceed on his chosen path with scarcely a backward glance. While most people might reconsider a decision made to leave home in the heat of a quarrel on the previous day, he is resolute. His journey to the cottage which he has decided to take, by way of contrast, shows nature in another of its moods; the sensitivity Hardy shows in describing a stormy day in June is as remarkable as the comparison of Tamsin to a series of birds later in the chapter.

Mrs Yeobright too can cut off her right hand with resolution, though the reader is able, through Hardy's comments and Tamsin's visit, to gain some idea of what it costs her to do so. Tamsin is able to see this and to comment on it objectively. The fact that she has married more out of a sense of duty than because of any great affection is borne out when we gather that her own married life, after only six months, seems less than ideally happy.

At the end of the chapter Wildeve's reaction to the news of Eustacia's approaching wedding is a reminder that marriage has in no way ended his philandering tendencies.

spade-guineas Coined between 1787 and 1799; the shield bearing the coat-of-arms was shaped like a pointed spade.
Ulysses His wanderings while returning home from the Trojan War are the subject of Homer's *Odyssey*.
Rousseau A French philosopher (1712–78) whose unorthodox ideas about government and conduct bore fruit in the French Revolution.

Chapter 7

Clym and Eustacia are married, but as in Wildeve's and Tamsin's case, their wedding is reported by a witness. Mrs Yeobright has refused to attend. She has a visit from Wildeve, who hints at Tamsin's pregnancy, and further mentions some article that she was expecting. Mrs Yeobright will not send the money with him, but she does later entrust it to Christian Cantle, who promises to deliver one bag to Tamsin at the Quiet Woman and the other to Clym at Alderworth. Christian gambles Mrs Yeobright's guineas away to Wildeve, and just as Wildeve is going to start from home the reddleman appears.

Commentary

The next two chapters contain one of the most memorable episodes of the novel. This is partly because of the strangeness and vividness of the events; but it is also because they exhibit a large measure of Hardy's fatalistic view of the world. The narrative also manages to include all three levels of Egdon society. The title of Chapter 7 – 'The morning and evening of a day' – seems a purposeful and extreme understatement.

At first Mrs Yeobright's studied pose can elicit little sympathy. The inflexible nature that has lost her her son and will not allow her to go to his wedding, also causes her continually to mistrust Wildeve – perhaps with more justification. The choice of Christian to carry the guineas is scarcely credible; but his behaviour in putting them into his boots, and the transparent naivety that proclaims that he carries a secret, are quietly amusing. The gathering of the heath-folk in the hollow and in the Quiet Woman is entirely convincing; and the reader might easily miss the subtle reintroduction of Venn. Wildeve's stratagem, by which he obtains the guineas, makes him appear almost Satanic, particularly as the scene returns to the darkness of the opening chapters with just the light of the horn-lantern to give it focus. The tension as Cantle loses the guineas that are not his is compelling – and just the place to end an episode.

fifty in each A large sum. In 1830 an agricultural labourer would have taken eighteen months to earn as much.
the Pitt diamond Thomas Pitt (1653–1726), an East India merchant, obtained the famous diamond named after him and is said to have sent it to England concealed in the heel of his son's shoe.
packman Pedlar (who carries a pack). Also known as a chapman.
caul The membrane covering the head of some babies at birth, credited by superstitious people as rendering them proof against drowning.
pair-royal Three dice of the same denomination.

Chapter 8

The reddleman gambles with Wildeve for his guineas and wins them all. He lets Clym go by after the wedding party and gives all the money to Thomasin.

Commentary

The events of this chapter are more poetic than realistic. They are memorable for the natural descriptions of the dell where the strange game takes place; of the insects that fly against the light; of the mute audience of heath-croppers; and of the glow-worms that provide the light for the last part of the game. Venn's ironic echoing of Wildeve's earlier persuasion of Christian helps to give him that faintly supernatural impression that he so frequently gives out. Hardy provides a convenient link with the story as it develops in the next section – and a melodramatic allusion to it – by making Venn innocently give all of the money to Thomasin.

pair, raffle of aces Terms in dicing. A pair is two dice of the same denomination, as a pair royal is three. A raffle of aces is a throw of three.

diorama A picture (or an exhibition of pictures) skilfully illuminated and viewed through the opening in the wall of a darkened room.

death's head moth A species of hawk-moth, whose pale markings can, with some imagination, be said to resemble a skull and crossbones.

Revision questions on Book 3

1 Account for the mutual fascination felt by Clym and Eustacia.

2 How is the conflict developed between Clym and his mother?

3 What use does Hardy make of rustic characters in this section?

4 To what extent are Hardy's descriptions in Book 3 poetic?

5 How much use does Hardy make of dialogue in this section, and to what effect?

6 'The scene of the gambling for the guineas is crude and unrealistic.' Do you agree?

Book 4, Chapter 1

After three or four weeks of complete happiness, Yeobright resumes his reading, and causes the first doubts in Eustacia, who up to then had never doubted her power to persuade him to return to Paris.

Mrs Yeobright is worried that she has received no acknow-ledgment of the money which she supposed had gone to Clym. At length Christian admits that he gambled away the money, and Mrs Yeobright goes to see Eustacia, meeting her at the pool and bank so familiar to the reader, near her grandfather's cot-tage. She asks Eustacia if she has received a gift of money from Wildeve, and Eustacia interprets this as a slur on her good name. There follows a bitter argument between them.

Commentary

As the year comes round to high summer, Clym and Eustacia enjoy the summer of their relationship, and their differences of character seem unimportant. Mrs Yeobright and Clym have what Hardy calls 'undeviating' characters, and while he pursues his studies his mother is led to the encounter to which the novel has been leading. It could have taken place already with Thomasin had she been made of sterner stuff. Eustacia is not the sort of person to ignore a real or imagined insult, and as a result, the central part of the novel – the conflict between son, wife and mother – approaches its dramatic climax.

Rencounter A subtle choice of words by Hardy. The word is close in sound to 'encounter' – a meeting; but the addition of the initial 'r' changes the meaning to that of a hostile meeting between adversaries.

Chapter 2

Clym grieves at the quarrel betwen his wife and his mother, and Eustacia pleads to be taken away from the Heath to Paris, saying that she does not mind how humbly they live.

Clym's studies far into the small hours lead to eye trouble; he has to give them up and take instead to furze and turf cutting. This he does with no sense of social failure, but to Eustacia his work is degrading.

Commentary

As both Clym and Eustacia see their hopes frustrated, the reader is led to compare their different reactions; Eustacia appears the less creditable of the two as her disappointment is the greater. If she has overestimated her power to bring her husband under her control, he has totally ignored her hatred of the Heath and all it stands for. The situation brings out a side of Clym that is typical of many Hardy characters: he rushes into misfortune and seems determined to enjoy it. And Hardy's marvellous description of Clym's fusion with nature shows that he (Hardy) shared his attitude. To take up an occupation dignified by antiquity, to become one with the landscape and to wear the uniform of a furze-cutter fulfils his deepest being – and he is relentlessly single-minded in its pursuit. In Eustacia he has met his match, and her unyielding nature is set to increase the conflict.

ophthalmia Inflammation of the eye.

Rasselas A fascinating novel written in great haste by Samuel Johnson (1709–1784) in 1759, in which he sets down not only his own ideas about the world, but those of the civilization of which he was such a representative figure. Here, a would-be inventor tried out a flying-kit, and though his wings would not sustain him in the air, they succeeded in doing so in the water into which he had fallen.

'Le point du jour . . .' From Act 2, Sc 8 of *Gulistan*, a comic opera by Charles-Guillaume Étienne, presented in 1805 and revived in 1844. It means:

Daybreak
Gives back to our thickets all their beauty
Flora is more beautiful at its return
The bird resumes its soft song of love
Everything in nature celebrates
Daybreak

Daybreak
Causes sometimes, causes extreme pain
How short the space of night is
For the shepherd burning with love
Forced to leave what he loves
At daybreak!

Chapter 3

Clym accepts his affliction stoically and is much more cheerful about it than is Eustacia. To lighten her depression she goes one afternoon to a 'gipsying' at a neighbouring village. There by accident she meets Wildeve, dances with him, and immediately revives old emotions. He takes her most of the way home. They see Clym, accompanied by the reddleman, coming to meet Eustacia; Wildeve makes off, but not before Venn has seen him. Venn goes quickly to the Quiet Woman and arrives there before Wildeve; at the inn he tells Thomasin that he has seen Wildeve leading a horse on the way home. The double meaning is clearly seen by Wildeve, who now knows that his meeting with Eustacia is no longer a secret.

Commentary

While the reunion of Wildeve and Eustacia is a coincidence, it is enough to rekindle a flame in each, an indication of how little conventional morality has affected either. Their meeting is set against the vivid description of a village fair, with the costumes of the dancers giving a splash of colour. It is a pointer towards the insularity of the heath-folk that neither Wildeve nor Eustacia seems to be recognized by anyone, though they are only six miles from home. There is a rare erotic quality in the description of their physical contact as it grows dark.

Venn is the will o' the wisp of *The Return of the Native*; the faint hint of preternatural ability is here maintained by his sudden reappearance after a retirement lasting for two chapters; by his amazing eyesight; by his ability to hurry over the dark heath by moonlight; and by a sophisticated use of words that can leave Wildeve in no doubt that he has been seen while Venn is protecting the naive Tamsin from that knowledge.

the St Lazarus . . . leper From Luke 16, 19–31, which, however, does not state that the sores of the beggar Lazarus were those of a leper. Leprosy was common in medieval England, and lepers had to carry a bell warning people of their approach. Clym is saying that his occupation makes him a social outcast.
braids Cf. Thomasin's braided hair, Book 2,8.
ophicleide A large bass trumpet, now largely obsolete.
wideawake The name for a soft felt hat worn in the 1850s.

Chapter 4

Wildeve comes to Alderworth and uses some of the signals he had used before to communicate with Eustacia, only to be checked at each move by Diggory Venn. Venn persuades Mrs Yeobright to call on Clym and Thomasin; simultaneously Clym decides to visit his mother and, while not actively supporting him, Eustacia agrees to put nothing in his way.

Commentary

Venn has always been a moral force; that morality is here brought into active effect against Wildeve. This use has a considerable comic content, as in the trip cord, the diversionary knocking at the door and the warning shot fired into the air, all of which are calculated to exasperate Wildeve as much as they are intended to set physical obstacles in his way or to harm him. The moth that flies into the flame is an image which Hardy uses in several places (see also his poem, 'The Moth Signal'), and here its purpose is partly symbolic. The narrator returns to the fore as the discomfited philanderer tries vainly to find the constable, only for Hardy instinctively to return to direct speech as first Mrs Yeobright, then Clym, decides to reopen lines of communication.

coup-de-Jarnac i.e. a crafty, underhand blow; named after the Seigneur de Jarnac, who in his duel before Henri II of France (10 July 1547) gave his opponent a sudden and unexpected blow (*coup*) and was declared the winner of the contest.

the impeachment of Strafford . . . Virginia Strafford was impeached on a variety of charges, lodged in the Tower and later executed (1641). Farmer Lynch was a Virginian planter and JP who, in 1780, realized that sending a company of loyalists to a regular court would mean their escape or rescue on the roads. He took the law into his own hands and decreed summary punishment, which was later legalized by special act.

Chapter 5

On a very hot August day Mrs Yeobright walks to Clym's house. The thought that a furze-cutter before her is her son bursts upon her just before he enters the door. As she rests on a little hill in view of the cottage she sees a second man, hesitating, who scans the house and garden, then goes in.

Commentary

This starts the episode in *The Return of the Native* that any reader will remember, and Hardy signals its importance with some of his most remarkable descriptions: of Egdon in high summer; the effect of summer on the vegetation; the contrasting effect of the Devil's Bellows; the distant view of Clym on his way home. The pause for Mrs Yeobright to rest is dramatically necessary, as it gives Clym time to fall asleep; but the whole section is suffused with ill-omen as, notwithstanding its happy ending, the impulse of this novel is mainly tragic.

when loose spokes ... carriages As the heat, which had dried them out, had caused them to contract and become loose.
the gait of Ahimaaz ... watchman of the king See 2 Samuel 18,27.
the birthplace of Shakespeare ... Hougomont i.e. a place of particular interest. Mary Stuart was Mary, Queen of Scots who, in 1568, fled from Scotland and put herself under the protection of Queen Elizabeth of England, only to find herself imprisoned in a succession of castles until her execution nearly twenty years later. The Château of Hougomont was a farm on the battlefield of Waterloo, which Hardy had visited two years before the novel was published.

Chapter 6

Having been at work since 4.30 a.m. Clym falls asleep immediately he reaches home. The caller seen by Mrs Yeobright is Wildeve. Wildeve is talking to Eustacia when Mrs Yeobright knocks. Eustacia looks through the window, sees who it is, and shows Wildeve out through the back door, thinking that Clym, whom she has just heard stirring, would waken and would open the door to his mother. By the time she realizes that no one has been let in, Mrs Yeobright has gone.

Commentary

It is important that Eustacia should not entirely lose the sympathy of the reader. The meeting and conversation with Wildeve shows her as honourable in intention, in not succumbing to temptation to conduct an extra-marital affair; and that in taking no account of her aspirations Clym is less than the completely caring husband. Her failure to open the door to Mrs Yeobright is emphasized as purely accidental, and Clym's saying 'Mother' at the crucial moment is yet another manifestation of Hardy's belief that fate uses man as a plaything – another in a collection of coincidences that directly affect the outcome of the novel.

As Mrs Yeobright starts her journey home, Johnny Nunsuch is used to give the scene added pathos by the naivety of his questions set against the melodrama of her assertions about Clym – and from the narrator an account of her walk that seems overtly sentimental. Johnny Nunsuch is of course a device; he seems several years younger than the boy who kept the fire ablaze for Eustacia earlier. The journey back gives Hardy more opportunity for natural observation – one notes the symbolism of the ants and of the heron: the one toiling instinctively for reasons they cannot comprehend; the other burnished in light as a token of man's aspirations, which he is never likely to attain.

Chapter 7

Clym had been made to dream by the knocking of his mother, and as soon as he wakes he sets off to see her. Eustacia says nothing to him of her visit. On the way he finds his mother lying exhausted on the heath. He carries her some way, and goes for help when he is nearly a mile from her house. A doctor is sent for and villagers give what help they can. It is found that Mrs Yeobright has been bitten by an adder, and an old wives' cure is applied.

Commentary

Clym's dream is pure melodrama. Eustacia's failure to tell him of his mother's visit is through embarrassment and a desire not to present herself in an unfavourable light. Ultimately it is to damage their marriage more than any other event. For the ending of the chapter the tone changes under the influence of the chorus; the world of the nightjar and the miller-moth is exchanged for that of repartee and folk-remedy, and the sense of tragedy is increased by the contrast between them.

white miller-moths Flour-coloured moths.
like Aeneas with his father Aeneas carried his father Anchises on his
  shoulders from the burning city of Troy.
nightjars Birds resembling swifts in appearance, with a characteristic
  'churring' call; they hunt for insects at night.
after I joined the locals in four His insistent boast: see 2,6; 3,7 and 6,4.

Chapter 8

Eustacia goes out to meet Clym on his return. As she is leaving, her grandfather calls to tell her that Wildeve has come into a large fortune. She meets Wildeve again on the heath, and he says that he did not tell her of his fortune at midday as it would have been greatly out of place to do so. He plans to travel all round the world, with a long stay in Paris.

They see light and a stir about the turf hovel; then keeping to the dark side of the hut they see the death of Mrs Yeobright — from exhaustion the doctor says. Johnny Nunsuch tells of her last words to him, to Clym's great distress, and Eustacia slips away.

Commentary

Captain Vye's visit shows him more talkative than he has been since his meeting with Venn in the second chapter, and he displays little tact in the way he rubs salt into the wound of his granddaughter's misfortune. If she is the willing object of Wildeve's visits, her behaviour here seems reasonably correct, though perhaps it is pride that makes her so little envious of his plans.

Their stumbling on the hut where Mrs Yeobright is dying presents the scene from an unexpected point of view. It emphasizes Eustacia's feeling of guilt at the death of her mother-in-law; and once again a crucial scene of the novel takes place in darkness. As the drama becomes more intense one notes how much Hardy's chapter-headings are extreme understatements of the events that take place in them. They are good examples of his sardonic sense of humour, and are often used in a double sense; here the 'Closed Door' is the door of Clym's cottage, but it is also the door of his relationship with his mother which, despite all his and her efforts, remains closed.

Revision questions on Book 4

1 Examine the clash of temperaments between Eustacia and Mrs Yeobright as they are developed in this section.

2 How does Clym's illness affect his behaviour and his outlook on life?

3 How far does Hardy emphasize the moral aspects of Wildeve's revived love for Eustacia?

4 'Egdon in summer is as forbidding as Egdon in winter.' Do you agree?

5 'As the novel proceeds, the character of Diggory Venn becomes increasingly remote from reality.' How far is this true?

6 Is the treatment of Mrs Yeobright's walk sentimental?

Book 5, Chapter 1

It is three weeks since the death of Clym's mother. He has been demented for a week, calm for four days, and since then in remorseful despair. Eustacia has said nothing to him yet of the door left shut against his mother, and Wildeve cautions her, if she does mention it, to keep back the fact that he was in the house.

Commentary

The language of the introductory paragraph is faintly archaic with its 'came forth from within', perhaps appropriately as the tone of the first few pages sustains the melodrama of the novel. Clym seems paradoxically almost to enjoy punishing himself in remorse for what logic would say is as much his mother's fault as his own – for at this stage he knows nothing of her arrival at Alderworth.

The most severe Victorian puritan, had he thought it right to read novels at all, must have thought that Clym's self-flagellation is more than sufficient penance. Thomasin's arrival is a breath of fresh air – it is surprising that there is only the faintest allusion to her by now advanced pregnancy. Wildeve's clandestine conversation with Eustacia reminds the reader that at some stage Clym is likely to discover the truth.

Wherefore is Light given . . . Misery Job 3, 20.
as the trial scene was to Judas Iscariot When he saw that Jesus was condemned he went and hanged himself. See Matthew 27, 3–5.
a Black Hole Referring to the 'Black Hole' of Calcutta, 20.7 metres square, into which 146 Europeans were thrust one night in 1756. All but 23 were suffocated by the next morning.
'Beware the fury of a patient man' From Dryden's *Absalom and Achitophel*, line 1005 (1681).

Chapter 2

A month later Clym goes to clear up at his mother's house, now his. Venn calls, not having heard of his mother's death, and tells him that, on his advice, Mrs Yeobright was certainly coming to see her son. Clym spends the night and the next morning there. Distressed and anxious to know more, he goes to see the boy who had walked on the heath with his mother before she died, Johnny Nunsuch. Johnny tells him that Mrs Yeobright had been to his house at Alderworth, that another man had gone in, that a lady had noticed that there was a caller but had not opened the door.

Commentary

The tone varies considerably in this chapter. It starts with Clym's gradual return to health, and two parallel incidents. The first of these is apparently cheerful, with the entry of Christian Cantle; but his announcement of the birth of Thomasin's daughter is a preface to Clym's main concern, which is an investigation into the circumstances of his mother's death. The second is the opening up of Blooms-End, again slightly melancholy with its meditations on the future of the family furniture, spiders' webs and dead flowers – lightened by the arrival of the reddleman. The climax, prepared with a characteristic example of sympathetic background in the chill atmosphere that Clym suddenly encounters, leads us to Susan Nunsuch's cottage. The scene immediately becomes dramatic and soon melodramatic. But the melodrama here is nearly all in Clym, and the Nunsuch household gives it its realistic base.

like Famine and sword From the anger and fury of the Lord God of hosts, as spoken by the prophet Jeremiah, if the people, the remnant of Judah, sought to enter into Egypt (Jeremiah 42, 16–17).

the Ascension . . . on the base Bible scenes – the ascension of Christ into heaven (Luke 24, 50–51; Acts 1, 9–11) and the miraculous draught of fishes (Luke 5, 4–11; John 21, 4–14).

dumb-waiter A stand with a revolving top for holding different dishes – common in Victorian households.

carking Distressing, causing anxiety.

toilets Processes of dressing.

who had behaved so barbarously to Eustacia When she stuck the stocking-needle into her (Book 3, Ch.2).

Oedipus In Greek mythology he discovered that he had unwittingly killed his father and married his mother.

Chapter 3

When he returns home Clym scourges Eustacia with his tongue about the discovery that he has made, at first passionately, then with more method. Eustacia prepares to leave, intending to return to her grandfather's. A message is received that Thomasin intends to call her baby daughter Eustacia Clementine, and Clym can only see this as a bitter comment on his failed marriage.

Commentary

In what is perhaps the most powerful purely dramatic episode in the book, Eustacia retains a good deal of her poise despite the relentless assault that Clym makes on her. The reader after all knows that her failure to open the door to Mrs Yeobright was more an accident than an intentional snub. Clym, however, is very ready to believe the worst of his wife, and in the way he calls her 'madam' and 'mistress' he is talking as if to a naughty child.

In magnifying Mrs Yeobright's virtues and minimizing her defects, Clym shows that the influence of his mother is greater than Eustacia's can ever be. In the process Eustacia comes as close as she ever does to achieving tragic stature. The proud girl of the early chapters cannot win the reader's sympathy, but the ambitious and talented girl stagnating on the heath in a remote cottage can do so.

Chapter 4

Eustacia goes back to her grandfather's house, only to find that he has gone away for the day and that the house is shut up. Charley is still there, and he climbs into the house, prepares a meal and lights fires for her. He also quietly removes two pistols at which he had noticed her looking closely. Her grandfather returns and receives her back without asking any questions.

Commentary

Eustacia's return to her grandfather's house is the more melancholy as the house is empty when she gets there. Charley has grown up from the lad who wanted to hold her hand in instalments; his attitude to her is unique among the characters of the novel, and comes close to veneration. But it is an admiration that is constructive and purposeful, and his removal of the pistols shows intelligence and initiative. Hardy wishes to include him at the same social level as the rustics; there is little doubt that they are the happiest beings in the novel, far more so than the petty aristocracy who are at the centre of the narrative.

between the dying ferns . . . webs Compare Clym's entry to his mother's cottage in Chapter 2.
transportation i.e. to Australia as a criminal.

Chapter 5

Charley worships Eustacia. It is the fifth of November and he lights a bonfire on the bank, in an attempt to give her the pleasure she had felt in previous years. As before, it succeeds in summoning Wildeve. He feels pity for her, and his pity brings her to tears. He offers assistance, and she agrees to signal one evening at eight o'clock when she wishes to escape. He promises to drive her to Budmouth, as the first stage in what she hopes will be a journey to France (and Paris).

Commentary

The year that has elapsed since the opening shows a Heath that is unchanged, but human beings that have changed a great deal. Eustacia especially is a chastened figure compared with the girl of twelve months before. Two typical Hardy effects are here clearly visible. The first is his use of coincidence, where the first time Eustacia uses her grandfather's telescope she chooses the occasion when Clym is moving the furniture to Blooms-End. The second is his sense of irony, as active as ever. The bonfire is intended by Charley to rekindle Eustacia's spirits. It does so in a way he does not expect, and though her walk towards it is at first perfunctory, Wildeve's arrival gradually revives her intensity. Up to now she has drawn back when tempted to break her marriage vows, and she disclaims any intention of doing so; but the end of the chapter sees a signal change in her in that she is brought to contemplate elopement.

Chapter 6

Time softens Clym's anger and he begins to want Eustacia back. She does not come, and he writes her a letter pleading with her, but in no way apologizing for what he has done. He resolves to send it the next day if she does not come within twenty-four hours. When Wildeve comes back from his bonfire-night visit to Eustacia, Thomasin mildly challenges him, but he decides to speak no more about it to her.

Commentary

Clym broods on his behaviour towards Eustacia against a background of humdrum garden tasks, which he needs to do to keep himself occupied. Thomasin is the quiet peacemaker who listens and gently suggests ways out of his problem; and if we find Clym's letter to Eustacia a little patronizing and self-righteous, this is echoed later by Wildeve's treatment of Thomasin, and is no more than a reflection of an age in which it was generally assumed that the man was master of the household.

Chapter 7

Eustacia gives her signal to Wildeve. The letter comes for her from Clym, and thinking she has gone to bed, her grandfather puts it on the mantelpiece until morning. Just before midnight Eustacia leaves her grandfather's home, but not without his hearing her. Her unpractical mind suddenly realizes that she is without money, and that to break her marriage vow for Wildeve is compromising herself in a way she would not have contemplated a year before.

The last section of the chapter gives an example of crude witchcraft on Egdon Heath as practised by Susan Nunsuch.

Commentary

The letter that is delivered just too late to have any effect is a device Hardy repeats in several of his novels. Here the failure is a triple one: first, when Captain Vye thinks Eustacia asleep and puts the letter on the mantelpiece; next when he thinks to deliver it as he sees the light from her room; and lastly when he calls to her to tell her of it just after she has left. Her journey towards Wildeve is again a highly atmospheric one, and is yet another of the important events that take place at night.

The image comparing the fungi to the liver and lungs of a colossal animal is particularly memorable, as are the evocations of chaos that follow it. When we hear that the wings of her soul were broken, there follows an episode that reveals Eustacia as full of self-pity. The reader may have some pity for her complaint, but equally the soliloquy reveals the selfishness that has been a prominent cause of her constant dissatisfaction, and which prevents her from ever becoming a truly tragic figure. Hardy took evident delight in the exactitude with which he describes Susan Nunsuch's attempts to maim and burn Eustacia's effigy, and it is a paradox that in the process she gets closer to witchcraft than Eustacia ever does.

posset A drink whose basis is hot milk.
the last plague of Egypt . . . Gethsemane The last plague of Egypt was the death of all the first-born of the Egyptians (Exodus 12, 29–30); Sennacherib was the King of Assyria of whose host the angel of the Lord smote 185,000 men as they lay in camp (2 Kings, 19,35); Christ's agony in the Garden of Gethsemane is told in Matthew 23, 36–46.

Chapter 8

Thomasin and not Eustacia calls to see Clym that night. She fears that Wildeve and Eustacia are going to run off together. Then Captain Vye comes with the news that Eustacia has gone from his house. Clym leaves Thomasin inside and makes for the Quiet Woman.

Meanwhile Thomasin cannot rest and leaves Blooms-End for home. She gets lost, but is fortunate enough to come across Diggory Venn, who shows her the way. He mentions that another woman has been around five minutes before. Near the Quiet Woman they see a light and make for it.

Commentary

Were it not for Hardy's attention to detail, the start of this chapter could be called Gothic. The darkness, the storm, the rattling window-panes and ivy brushing against them are all conventional Gothic paraphernalia. But the chapter is enriched by the author's architectural knowledge and made more convincing by human beings who are believable. As the climax approaches, most of the main characters are brought together at Blooms-End, and as first Clym then Thomasin attempt to walk through the storm to the Quiet Woman, the reddleman is brought back. His van and his lively colour mark a haven in the darkness; his observation of 'another woman' who has passed by increases our curiosity, and his intimate knowledge of the heath reassures us that virtue may yet triumph.

quarries Diamond-shaped pieces of glass held together by strips of grooved lead.
Saint Sebastian A Christian martyr shot to death by arrows. He was the subject of several famous paintings.

Chapter 9

The wanderers are drawn together by the lights of Wildeve's gig. Wildeve half hopes to accompany Eustacia abroad, but as Clym comes up, the fall of a body into the adjoining weir is heard. Both Wildeve and Venn jump into the swollen river to attempt a rescue, but Eustacia and Wildeve are drowned. Clym feels that he has been responsible for the deaths of two women.

Commentary

In Hardy's original conception of the novel, this was the last chapter. For it the omniscient author returns, who knows all Wildeve's intentions and his motives. It is fitting that the action should take place in the middle of the night and that there should be a strong element of confusion in this story where the fates combine to frustrate so many plans; it is also an example of sympathetic background, where the weather and the circumstances closely fit the mood of the surrounding narrative. That it should be Venn who salvages what is possible from the weir is fitting, given his role in the rest of the story.

The deaths of Wildeve and Eustacia make a convenient ending to the novel; the description of the dead bodies laid out in the bedrooms of the Quiet Woman manages to preserve the youth and spark that is so much part of them, and in which Clym is relatively wanting. Clym's readiness to lacerate himself appears yet again, and it requires the calmness of Venn to restore an element of balance.

packet A ship plying regularly between one port and another, carrying passengers, packets of letters etc.
hartshorn Ammonia – a principal ingredient of smelling-salts.
looking like Lazarus . . . tomb See John 11, 41–6. The Lazarus is the brother of Mary and Martha, not the beggar mentioned on p.50.
scarified Marked with scars.

Revision questions on Book 5

1 To what extent does Eustacia deserve to be blamed for the events of this section of the novel?

2 'For one who wishes to be a moral force on Egdon, Clym Yeobright is far too unforgiving.' Do you agree?

3 How far does Hardy make excessive use of melodrama in this section?

4 What use does Hardy make of darkness in this section?

5 'Hardy would have improved *The Return of the Native* by concluding it at the end of Book 5.' Do you agree?

Book 6, Chapter 1

Eighteen months afterwards Thomasin is at Blooms-End, with Clym living in part of the house separately and frugally. The maypole festivities are held that year at Blooms-End, but Thomasin, as an unattached woman, could not and Clym would not join in. When they are over, Venn, now a respectable dairyman, stays behind to look for a glove dropped by one of the maidens.

Commentary

The content of the last book was forced on Hardy by the demands of the public and of his publisher, and the style is notably heavier than it has been since the very first part of the novel. Clym's reflections on fortune are a good deal less emphatic than Eustacia's were, and his ascetic nature makes his lot a relatively enjoyable one for him. His plans for educating the heath-folk have been driven into abeyance by his troubles with his sight; but even so we might reasonably have been reminded of them as an expression of his frustration. His experiences seem to have aged him to an extent that is surprising in one who is barely thirty.

Thomasin is the pivot of normality in the chapter, and Diggory Venn, who in every sense is paler than on his previous appearances, and who starts to court her anew, does so in a springtime atmosphere that was less in evidence the last time spring was mentioned in Book 3, 5. Venn's assiduity in looking for the lost glove would perhaps be comic were it not to be revealed as part of yet another plan.

a first Cause i.e. an omnipotent God deliberately creating the world, as in the first chapter of Genesis.
while they sit down . . . Babylon A reference to Psalm 137, where the captives in their sorrow still think of Jerusalem as above their chief joy, and do not renounce their religion as having led them into oppression.
Teutonic Belonging to an ancient northern race, which helped to people Germany, England and Scandinavia.
ragged-robins Red campions.

Chapter 2

Thomasin finds out that the glove for which Venn was out looking was her own – borrowed by one of the maids for the maypole evening. One day when she sees him on the Heath she asks him for it, and he takes it immediately from his breast-pocket. They exchange reserved but not unpleasing words.

Commentary

The social status of Thomasin at the end of the novel has been considerably raised by the wealth she has inherited from her husband. Mrs Yeobright had clearly looked on herself as a degree or so above her neighbours in standing, and the possession of three servants makes the household almost part of the Heath's minor gentry. The saga of the glove becomes a symbol of Venn's constancy, amid wryly observed comments on Thomasin's growing child.

Chapter 3

Clym is wondering whether to propose to Thomasin out of a sense of duty to fulfil a dead mother's hope. She unwittingly prevents him from doing so by telling him that she is thinking of marrying Venn. In deference to his mother's view and to his own regarding Venn's position, he is at first unenthusiastic, but Thomasin is obviously convinced that her aunt would have thought him a fitting husband now, and Clym is content. The wedding is fixed.

Commentary

Hardy's disclaimer at the end of this chapter that the original conception of the story did not end with Thomasin marrying Venn is plain well before one reaches it. The present ending appears contrived, and nowhere more than here. Clym is given a touch of self-interest, then a balancing touch of remorse. It becomes plain that the root of Mrs Yeobright's and Thomasin's earlier objections to Venn as a suitor (and initially Clym's) derive from differences of social class, and particularly from the supposedly demeaning effect of making a living from selling reddle.

Social class and its effects was a lifelong obsession of Hardy's; that Fairway should come in at the end and give voice to what Clym has been privately thinking is a dramatic device to make him disclaim any such thought – and perhaps a comment on the general lack of ambition among the heath-folk.

the eleventh commandment Christ's commandment: 'Thou shalt love thy neighbour as thyself.'
In the words of Job Job 31,1.

Chapter 4

Thomasin is married to Venn. Clym asks to be excused from the festivities, and on the heath meets Charley, who requests a memento of Eustacia. Clym gives him a lock of her hair. Events have borne out for Clym the accuracy of his mother's judgement, and he wants to live his life again.

On the following Sunday Clym can be seen on the top of Rainbarrow; he has found his vocation – to be an itinerant preacher.

Commentary

What might easily have been a sentimental ending is avoided by the use of the rustic chorus for the first time since Mrs Yeobright's death. They are once more presented in a very memorable way, making a feather-bed for Venn and Thomasin. Hardy's sense of humour is concentrated in them, and the atmosphere is thereby lightened considerably. Frivolity, however, even at a wedding, would be an inappropriate way to end a novel about Egdon, as Hardy has characterized it. The reminders of Eustacia, Clym's melancholy manner, and the final picture of the preacher on Rainbarrow are perhaps more in keeping.

bed-tick The covering part of a mattress in which the feathers were placed.

bruckle-hit A poor showing.

Candlemas-day 2 February, the feast of the Presentation of Christ in the Temple; children were given candles as Christ was 'a light to lighten the Gentiles'.

I'll go to 'em ... wedding-song, hey? As they did after the supposed wedding of Wildeve and Thomasin (1,5).

Old Midsummer night 13 June (instead of 24). New-style reckoning was instituted in 1752; rural Dorset keeps to the old ways nearly a century later.

the office at the wedding-service ... hands i.e. giving away the bride.

'And the king ... I will not say thee nay.' Solomon's words to his mother, Bath-shebah; and not a good illustration as he did say her nay and indeed slew the man for whom she asked a favour (1 Kings 2,20).

Revision questions on Book 6

1 Which of Hardy's two alternative endings do you find the more satisfactory?

2 'The Thomasin of the last book is as unrecognizable from the Thomasin of the rest of the novel as is Venn.' Is this true?

3 'The most interesting aspect of the last four chapters is the close observation of country customs.' Do you agree?

Hardy's art in *The Return of the Native*
The characters

Clym Yeobright

Mother, what is doing well?

Clym is the Native of the title who returns to the Heath where he has been brought up. His return is at first supposedly for a holiday, then we discover that in reality Clym's purpose is a deeply moral one. Though it is arguable whether he or Eustacia is the most important character in the novel, it is difficult to fault Hardy's technique in presenting him. In common with most tragic heroes he does not enter until quite some way into the story; there is a considerable build-up before he appears, and as the first two occasions take place in darkness, there is even an air of mystery comparable to that of Eustacia when she is first presented.

Clym is first described in artistic terms, and is compared to a Rembrandt picture. The intensity conveyed by such a comparison is just, in that Clym proves to be equally intense; in the second paragraph Hardy identifies his weakness as a tendency to think too much. There is a certain irony in this because the terms Hardy uses are uncompromisingly intellectual. Clym's questions to Eustacia in her disguise as the Turkish Knight are his first spoken words. They show him treating the disguised Eustacia with courtesy, sharply curious to know who this strange person is, yet happy not to pry further when he realizes that more questioning is likely to embarrass her. This side of Clym gradually disappears as his intentions become clearer, but it re-emerges in the last part of the story, where he keeps a tactful distance from Thomasin when she moves into Blooms-End.

What his mother admires about Clym is his prosperity. He has succeeded in her eyes since he has escaped from the limiting environment of Egdon; and one of the appeals of the book must have been to countless women who were desperate that their sons should not end up by marrying the village girls and be condemned to the same life of toil that they had themselves experienced. Clym's searching question to his mother: 'What is doing well?' sums up the clash in their contrasting ambitions, and prepares us for the parting of their ways that is to come soon afterwards.

For Eustacia, his attraction is subtly different. She too admires the escape he has made. But whereas the Egdon folk seem to think of Paris as 'a rookery of pomp and vanity' [where the violence of the French Revolution was still one of its compelling features], Eustacia looks upon it as the centre of the fashionable world. Clym has matured sufficiently during his stay there to see this as a mirage.

Yet the sober Clym falls for the first English girl with whom he comes into contact, and within three months of their first meeting they are married. This is surely not very sensible; but that is not all. His enthusiasm for the idea of starting up a school and his wish to do good to his fellow-creatures show an impracticable idealism; his conviction that he can change Eustacia's mind and redirect her ambitions into becoming an assistant in a school in Budmouth is almost arrogant. There is ample evidence here that Clym does not really know himself, and certainly does not know Eustacia. He is foolish not to see the life that she really wanted, and his intellectual approach is able to convince him that he is not marrying her merely because he desires her sexually.

Naturally when he finds that his mother and his lover are in conflict with one another, his lover wins, and he is single-minded in finding the cottage at Alderworth. He does not seek confrontation but he does little to avoid it, either with his mother, or later with his wife. It is at this juncture that Clym first has problems over his failing sight, which threaten his grand plan before it has got under way.

His reaction to this is instinctive and characteristic. In turning to cutting furze, working long hours, and doing it all so wholeheartedly, he is frustrating the ambitions of both his mother and his wife. He seems positively to enjoy the work; the song he sings is metaphorical as well as literal. The return of the native has been into an occupation as primitive as that of his ancestors. Far from being a liberated man, Clym treats Eustacia in a way not very different from that in which Wildeve treats Thomasin. When Eustacia has decided to return to her grandfather and is unable to tie her bonnet in the passion she feels, he offers to tie the strings for her, but 'turned his eyes aside that he might not be tempted to softness'. He has proved what Mrs Yeobright has said about him earlier, that he is as hard as steel; he is the true son of a mother who is herself unable to compromise.

There is indeed much of the puritan about Clym. He does not seem to enjoy studying but does so for a purpose, sitting enslaved over his books. Study for him is a means to an end, which shows a creditable determination. There is more than a touch of the fanatic about the way he tackles it, at a time when schoolmasters did not have to have any qualification. Similarly, he thinks that he will marry Thomasin as a duty to his departed mother. He knows her no better than he has known Eustacia, but still carries around with him the certainty that he is right. This is perhaps one of the reasons why he finds contentment in whatever he wishes to do.

Yet even at the end of the story there is little humility in Clym. His life as an itinerant preacher is based upon bringing the light to people like those who cluster round Rainbarrow to hear him. He is a barely past the age of thirty, yet he behaves like a biblical seer, something for which his experiences have ill-prepared him. He may be a sadder man than he was, but one may wonder whether he is a wiser one. If Hardy calls him 'the nicest of my heroes – and not a bit like me', one cannot think that he was being entirely serious.

Eustacia Vye

The heath is a cruel taskmaster to me

Eustacia first appears in the sixth chapter of *The Return of the Native*; Clym Yeobright has to wait until the seventeenth. This gives her a start from which he is never able to recover. In addition to this she has other advantages. She is enigmatic where he is transparent; strikingly beautiful where he is damaged by thinking too much; and full of raw romantic appeal where he is merely prosaic.

Her first appearance in the story must be among the most striking in fiction, seen as she is in the dark, climbing towards the top of Rainbarrow where she finds the dying embers of the fire that earlier had been such a beacon for miles around. Her absolute confidence is remarkable, and in huge contrast to all the characters that have been described before. She seems too startling a phenomenon to live on this desolate Heath, and the magnetic power she shows in drawing Wildeve to her, not to mention Charley and later Clym, is an indication that Hardy first thought of her in terms of witchcraft. The title of 'Queen of Night' given to her in the seventh chapter has a certain supernatural suggestion about it – Mozart had used it in *The Magic Flute* nearly a hundred years before, and the treatment given her by Susan Nunsuch survives as a relic of Hardy's original conception.

It is not surprising that when Hardy starts to explore the character, her impact diminishes somewhat. Though her background is exotic for Egdon – the daughter of a bandmaster from Corfu – her grandfather seems ordinary enough. Hardy took the name of the character from a lady who lived just to the south of Egdon, at Owermoigne, in the fifteenth century. Into Eustacia he put all his feelings about bewitching women. She is, at nineteen, fully aware of her power, fortunate in never having known a moment of physical suffering in her whole life, and anxious for a grand passion. She herself realizes that Wildeve is a man who is not cut out for such a role, but hangs on to him instinctively until she can find someone who suits her better.

Her behaviour over the mumming shows that she possesses initiative and an inborn sense of melodrama that exploits every situation in which she finds herself, from where she lies inert against the clock-case, to the drink taken through her visor, and in giving oblique answers to Clym when he asks her questions about herself.

Eustacia's positive reaction to Clym, which soon becomes courtship, is partly instinctive because his associations have made her half in love with him before he appears, and partly calculation in that she hopes it will provide the means by which she can escape from the Heath. She has always been different from everyone else, as they all recognize, in a state of rebellion against the predictable; now she marries Clym for what she can get out of marriage rather than what she can put into it. It is ironic, therefore, that this action ends up by attaching her more firmly to the Heath rather than helping her to escape from it.

Yet she is not without a certain integrity. At a time when the bonds of marriage were much stronger than they are now, the whole of her being is urging her to flout convention and do just what she wants to, but she shows that she is reluctant to elope with Wildeve. To Clym and to Diggory Venn she may be on the verge of committing adultery, but the reader knows that thought is not transferred into action. Even when she is on the verge of escaping to Budmouth with Wildeve, it is clear that her marriage vows mean something to her; if she accepts money from him she will have to allow him to accompany her, and she still considers him as inadequate. Her suicide is perhaps an attempt to escape from this impossible dilemma; if the world cannot provide her with the things that she really wants, to run away from it seems one solution.

Critics have been divided as to whether Eustacia is dignified or simply proud. The terms are very close in meaning, and perhaps it is fair to say that she is both. Her behaviour has the imperious quality of someone who has always had her own way. Her grandfather seems happy to leave her to her own devices. He shows no particular interest in anything she does, never takes her anywhere, keeps himself to himself and leaves her to get along as best she can. As a result she lives like one of the minor aristocracy – with a servant to do all the menial jobs about the house. She dominates Charley, Wildeve and Clym; the scene where Charley is allowed to hold her hand in instalments is at once amusing and a measure of how compelling is her dignity. But it changes easily into pride. She remains constantly jealous of Thomasin, before and after she marries Wildeve, declaring to Venn that she 'will not be beaten down by an inferior woman like her', and later telling Wildeve, 'She won you away from me and she deserves to suffer for it.'

It is relatively easy to retain dignity when one has something that other people want – in her case her position or her person. It is much harder to do so when one has nothing – and Eustacia finds herself in this position when she is married to Clym and living at Alderworth. Her humiliation is complete when her husband becomes a furze-cutter, and in her reaction she shows that her attitude is closer to that of Mrs Yeobright than she would have cared to admit. During Clym's illness she is apathetic, and it soon becomes clear that she has little idea of how to retain her dignity in poor circumstances. She manages to keep a servant and to get up late in the morning, but her attitude to Wildeve once he has come into his large fortune is one of jealousy. All these things are hallmarks of pride rather than of dignity.

In addition, Eustacia demonstrates her selfishness throughout the book. She marries Clym partly as an act of revenge upon

Wildeve when he has neglected her in favour of Thomasin. She is ready to use Wildeve as an outlet for her feelings: 'I determined you should come; and you have come! I have shown my power.' She is quite unconcerned that he should be kept waiting for her; she uses the bonfire as a peremptory summons and cares not at all who will be inconvenienced by it. Yet when the climax comes and she prepares to leave for France, she is filled with self-pity: 'I do not deserve my lot ... How hard it is of Heaven to devise such tortures for me, who have done no harm to Heaven at all!' As a result it is hard to feel unrelieved sympathy for her.

Hardy wrote *The Return of the Native* in full awareness of the classical theory of tragedy, which stated that the tragic hero should be someone like ourselves – neither wholly good nor wholly bad. One cannot easily feel for a person who is so self-centred. If Eustacia's upbringing has given her not enough to do and unreasonable expectations, one has more feeling for Thomasin, who seems to accept what life offers her. There is no doubt, however, that Eustacia is the most memorable character in the book, and one of the most memorable in nineteenth-century fiction, the more compelling because of the smouldering sexuality that lies just below the surface.

Diggory Venn

The well-known form in corduroy, lurid from head to foot

Venn is a strange mixture. There are relatively few developed characters in *The Return of the Native*, and Hardy uses him for a variety of purposes. The result is a human being who is not at all convincing, but whose interest lies in other directions.

As Hardy explains, Venn is an example of a dying breed. At the time he wrote the novel, reddlemen were more or less extinct, even on Egdon; but Hardy was writing about a period nearly forty years earlier, the time of his own childhood. In this supposedly timeless Heath, then, Diggory acts as something of a museum-piece, the presentation of a country figure who is preserved in the pages of this novel better than he could ever be in a museum. His lively colour so penetrates the pages that he is one of the characters whom anyone who has read the novel is likely to remember long after Wildeve and Clym are forgotten. His appearances, and as sudden disappearances, impart an air of mystery; and Hardy's original ending where Venn was intended to vanish into the Heath seems preferable to the pale figure who is resurrected for the revised ending.

His first appearance occurs under melodramatic conditions as he brings the compromised Thomasin home from Anglebury. We soon gather that his interest is personal in that he has long been an admirer of Thomasin, and before the story has opened he has proposed to her. She seems never to have considered him as a serious suitor, and we gather later that social class has been the main reason. Even so, she does not seem to be tempted to see him as anything other than a generous rescuer.

Venn, however, quickly gains the reader's admiration. With a vulnerable girl tucked away in his van he does nothing to take advantage of an unexpected opportunity; throughout the novel he is completely correct in his behaviour. In his attempt to persuade Eustacia to stop tempting Wildeve he is even willing to arrange a post for her in Budmouth; behaviour that goes beyond what could reasonably be expected. He is the guardian who warns Thomasin in oblique terms that Wildeve has an ulterior motive behind his nocturnal walks. His van is a haven of stability whenever it appears; one notices at the same time how closely Hardy has observed it, describing as he does the padlock with which Venn secures it, and, as the climax approaches, the pool of water that has fallen from Thomasin's cloak.

His other role is to be something of a supernatural agent. In this, he to some extent balances other examples of this element in the story – the crude witchcraft of Susan Nunsuch, for example. Venn seems always to be in the right place at the right time. Some of this is through design, as when he hears the meeting between Wildeve and Eustacia. But his entry to win back the guineas lost by Christian Cantle is uncanny; his walk over the heath in the dark to tell Thomasin of her husband's purchase of a horse is barely credible – as anyone who has tried to walk over an area of country when it is totally dark will bear witness. He might with some justice be called a *deus ex machina* – an agent, semi-divine, used to interfere in a story to make it end satisfactorily.

As we have seen, Hardy's original intention was to make Venn disappear into the Heath. If he had done so, we would have been left with the image of Thomasin trusting him to carry her baby on the wild night of her husband's death; of his pulling first

Clym, then Wildeve, then Eustacia out of the whirlpool beneath Shadwater Weir, and sitting in the Quiet Woman, the voice of sanity, as the company there starts to assimilate the events of the night.

The Venn of the last section seems quirky by comparison. His search for the glove by moonlight is close to being comic; the way he immediately produces the glove from near his heart when asked for it by Thomasin later seems equally so. As, newly respectable, he takes Thomasin off to church and to his dairy-farm in a dog-cart, one can feel that Hardy has given the story a sort of symmetry but that his heart is not in this ending.

Thomasin Yeobright

I am a practical woman now

Thomasin, or Tamsin as she is variously called, starts off the story of *The Return of the Native* in most compelling fashion. She is first presented asleep in Diggory Venn's van, and later we hear that she has run up to Venn saying that she is in trouble. This conjures up in the reader's mind problems that are considerably greater than those she is wanting to explain, and it is some time later that we learn the whole story. As a suffering maiden, hers is a passive role. She never gains a more active one because she is eclipsed by Eustacia; and with a Mrs Yeobright in the background, too, the story could not stand a character who is developed more than she is.

There is throughout a certain pathos about her. We hear nothing about her parents; she has been brought up by her aunt, and the degree of commitment that Mrs Yeobright shows to her is significantly less than it would have been were she her daughter. So when she has left to be married she is told later 'my power over your welfare came to an end when you left this house to go with him to Anglebury.' Her course has not been smooth – Mrs Yeobright has forbidden the banns when Thomasin has tried to get married once before; when she is eventually married Wildeve seems not to value his conquest as much as he might. The wedding, when it happens, is a quiet affair. Before it, Thomasin has hidden herself during the festivities at Blooms-End through embarrassment at her predicament. She has prepared for the ceremony by braiding her hair in sevens, but even so, when she has arranged for her cousin to be elsewhere when it happens, and when her aunt prefers not to attend the ceremony, it has to be seen as an anticlimax.

Married life gives her the job of helping to run an inn, a husband who is inconstant, and a pregnancy that immediately follows her marriage. Throughout Thomasin remains placid, not questioning her role in married life; and as her husband sees it, that role is to obey.

Her husband's newly inherited riches provide them with the possibility of a changed lifestyle, but she remains practical, and would no doubt have earned Victorian approval by being more interested in saving her money for her daughter.

Her attitude to the Heath is in stark contrast to that of Eustacia; she finds it a 'nice wild place to walk in'. She steadily increases in maturity as the story continues, is able to talk sensibly to her aunt about what Mrs Yeobright sees as an infatuation on the part of her son, and to come to consult Clym when she feels that Wildeve and Eustacia are about to elope.

The last section sees her a widow less than a year after her marriage. By then she seems entirely self-possessed and practical, knowing her own mind, and ready to marry Diggory Venn once she has discussed the matter with her cousin. Her second marriage seems likely to be happier than her first, but she can never be as interesting a character as Eustacia; as a result the ending of the novel seems something of an anticlimax.

Wildeve

You ... look at the Heath as if it were somebody's gaol

For one whose talents are no more than mediocre, Wildeve has astonishingly good luck. He has trained as an engineer, but has lacked either the perseverance or the ability to make his living at it, and has ended up in the relatively humble occupation of innkeeper. He is therefore a newcomer to the area of the Heath, and has no great affection for it. His function in the story is to provide the third side of the triangular relationship between himself, Eustacia and Thomasin, and as such he has to be made into a philanderer.

At this he seems successful. He is able to captivate Thomasin, and despite suffering the indignity of having the banns of his marriage forbidden by Mrs Yeobright, and the further blow of finding himself with a licence that is invalid, he is able to keep her on a string for a relatively long time. Their ultimate marriage is something of another anticlimax.

From the start, Diggory Venn has little time for him. This is partly because he has failed where Wildeve has succeeded – in gaining the hand of Thomasin – but it is also because Venn observes early that he 'notices the looks of women'. When Wildeve is drawn to Eustacia's fire and the affection between them springs again into life, it would seem another example of his power over women. But Eustacia is no ordinary woman and in her he has met his match. She covets him largely because there is nobody else of comparable character to attract her, and he is caught uncomfortably between the two of them until the arrival of Clym gives Eustacia metal more attractive. The fact that Wildeve marries Thomasin mainly to gain revenge on Eustacia shows another unattractive side to his character.

This is confirmed when a little later he notices that Christian Cantle has a secret. He is able to trick Christian into losing all the precious guineas at a game of dice; his intention is purely to get his own back on Mrs Yeobright, who has refused to entrust them to him. One cannot blame him in the context of the time for his stated belief that what is his wife's is his; one can blame him for keeping her short of money. He behaves haughtily towards Venn, considering himself a few rungs higher up the ladder of social status than a reddleman, and acting accordingly.

After Eustacia's marriage, the affair between them gradually comes to life again, partly through chance. It is an accident, for instance, that brings them together at the East Egdon fair, but he has clearly been anxious for some time to see her again. He finds an illicit love intriguing simply because it is illicit, and there seems to be plenty of evidence that even were he married to Eustacia, his roving disposition would not let him keep still for long. He trades on his wife's gentleness, treating her increasingly like a chattel as the story continues. When she is not treated as a chattel, Thomasin is treated as a child without a mind of her own. Wildeve is understandably devious when Venn has brought Thomasin an oblique account of his meeting with Eustacia; but the reader has little sympathy for him and enjoys his discomfiture here, and earlier when he trips over Venn's snares.

At this stage Wildeve inherits a large sum of money. While he is not immediately extravagant, he goes to see Eustacia at Alderworth, clad in a new summer suit and a light hat, which contrast sharply with Clym's leather leggings and gloves – and he does not mention his new fortune. When eventually the details emerge and Eustacia hears of his plans to travel widely, it must be said that he does not taunt her with telling her what they are – he has no need to do so.

The end of Book 5 finds Wildeve preparing to arrange Eustacia's flight to Paris. There is more than a hint that they intend to elope, as he takes a considerable sum of money with him, and has pressed her to agree to an elopement. His jump into the weir to save her is impulsive; his failure to remove his greatcoat must be considered one of the contributory factors to his death.

His role in the novel is ultimately unsatisfactory as he is used mainly to reveal more of Eustacia. This means that he is prevented from being an interesting character, and the reader ends up by agreeing with Eustacia – that he is not great enough for her to give herself to.

Mrs Yeobright

I have a burden which is more than I can bear

Mrs Yeobright is a curate's daughter. This seemingly unimportant piece of information in fact tells us a great deal about her behaviour throughout the novel, because it indicates that her social class is distinctly higher than that of the ordinary heathfolk. She owns her house and intermittently has a servant; the likes of Christian Cantle treat her with deference. At the same time Captain Vye can call the family countrified, because they sit in the kitchen and drink mead; they also sand the kitchen floor.

Before the story opens, her ambitious nature has sent her son to Paris, perhaps partly in the hope that his horizons will be widened enough to make money and to settle down well away from his roots. She has brought up her niece, and has disapproved of her marriage enough to forbid the banns in public. Such an action shows an attitude to life that is totally uncompromising; tact seems to be a word missing from her vocabulary.

At the beginning of story she meets the heath-folk, who tell her that the reddleman has been enquiring for her. They treat her with evident respect. Her question to Thomasin, asking what is the meaning of this disgraceful performance, makes no concession to any bruised feelings that her niece might have, and her mood swings quickly from sensitivity to harshness. She makes no secret of her dislike for Wildeve, either here or later. Her greatest slight to him, however, is her refusal to entrust him with the money that is destined for Thomasin; it must be said that her judgement is sound.

Over Venn's request to her for the hand of Thomasin Mrs Yeobright acts with diplomacy, realizing that it will give her a negotiating point, which she uses shrewdly. She then leaves the foreground. There are two memorable pictures of her taking apples down from the loft, and picking bunches of holly to decorate Blooms-End. In her desire for privacy, Thomasin does not ask her to her wedding. As she departs to be married, Mrs Yeobright throws a shoe at her, and this is as close to showing a sense of humour as she ever gets.

The second half of the novel is occupied by the triangular tussle between Mrs Yeobright, Clym and Eustacia. In the battle for the soul of Clym she cannot win. Her attempts to persuade him to return to Paris, to give up his highly moral ideas, and to see Eustacia with clarity, are doomed to failure because he is as stubborn as she is. The result is that she loses him. Her argument with Eustacia by the pool shows her speaking with more consideration and clarity than Eustacia does, but ineffectively. All the same, the dispute prevents her from ever speaking to her son again.

Mrs Yeobright's last appearance is the memorable one of her walk over the scorching heath. She is the victim here of fate; of the heat that means she is exhausted even before she arrives at Alderworth; of the chance arrival of Wildeve at the back door; of Clym's calling out in his sleep at the crucial time; and of Eustacia's failure to pursue her when she has gone. Her conversation with Johnny Nunsuch is one in which Hardy attempts to gain as much dramatic effect as possible out of the situation. As she dies in the hut, her personality ceases to have any effect on the story, except that of making Clym blame himself incessantly for what has happened. She has in this last appearance seemed like an old woman, and this must be judged part of Hardy's attempt to make the situation as moving as possible when we realize that she cannot be much more than fifty.

Minor characters

Hardy had used a group of country people as part of *Far from the Madding Crowd* to comment on the action. It was so successful that he did so again in *The Return of the Native*, and he was to use them repeatedly in his later novels, though the way he uses them becomes more sophisticated as he grows in experience.

The heath-folk of *The Return of the Native* are a vital ingredient of the story. They provide humour where all the main characters are painfully intense, and they comment on those characters in a way that gives the novel much more balance. It may be noted that Hardy was studying Greek drama not long before he wrote the book, and Greek drama makes extensive use of a Chorus to comment on the action of the main plot, though they take no active part in it. Greek drama uses the Chorus en masse, but Hardy adapts them to suit his purposes, and subtly differentiates his characters.

Grandfer Cantle is the village ancient. He is constantly talking about his youth, and the period of the Napoleonic War, when he joined the 'Bang-up Locals'. He is always ready for a drink and a song, one of the most prominent of the party that assembles to serenade what they think is the newly-married couple inside the Quiet Woman. He is able to dance, too, and if the others become tired of him they are more than ready to tell him so, something they are prevented from doing to the main characters; differences of class make it a step they instinctively refuse to take. So if Timothy Fairway tells Grandfer Cantle to stop singing as it is 'too much for the mouldy weasand of such a old man as you', he prefers to talk about Clym behind his back (Book 3,1).

His son *Christian* is the nearest the story gets to the village idiot, aged 31 last tatie digging, born when there was no moon, easily scared and who, having nothing else to distinguish him, likes to be noticed as the man whom no woman will marry. He acts as servant to Mrs Yeobright, and it is one of the more improbable features of the story that she entrusts a large sum of money to him to carry and deliver to two people on the other side of the Heath. His big round eyes make him look an idiot, and he applies the fatalism of a rustic to his own case: ''Twas to be if 'twas, I suppose. I can't help it, can I?'

Timothy Fairway, the turf-cutter, enjoys a lively dance with Susan Nunsuch at a bonfire festival. As the village barber, he provides free haircuts outside his house, and another opportunity for conversation. His enjoyment of 'a good hearty funeral as well as anything' is amusing. He thinks very little of Clym's grandiose schemes to keep a school in the locality, though again he does not say so to his face.

One of the most interesting is *Susan Nunsuch*, who at first appears to have no special features, but as the story gathers momentum appears rather more luridly as the local witch. In this she may have gathered some of the attributes originally meant for Eustacia [in Hardy's first conception of the story]. But her sticking the needle into Eustacia in church 'so as to draw her blood and put an end to the bewitching of Susan's children' makes her part of the pagan past of Egdon. Later she tries to damage her imagined adversary by making an effigy of her and sticking pins into it while she repeats the Lord's Prayer three times backwards. If Hardy exaggerates here, the element of horror, wildness and savagery he brings to the story is not inappropriate in the context of the Egdon he wished to portray.

Her son *Johnny Nunsuch* is something of a general-purpose character. He it is who feeds Eustacia's bonfire for her at the start, for what is perhaps, in the context of his mother's interests, the appropriate payment of a crooked sixpence. Later in the story he is nearly six miles away at Alderworth to see the arrival of Mrs Yeobright; to observe Eustacia looking out as she arrives; to provide Mrs Yeobright with a drink of water from the pond, and to enter into conversation with her. Without him, her last words would have been a soliloquy, and in the child's view of events that he gives, he stands closer to the person of the young Hardy than anyone else, for it must be remembered that Hardy himself was Johnny's age when the events he describes happened, and there is no doubt that in the magnification of distances, in the way quite small things seem large, Egdon Heath is seen with the memory of childhood.

The heath-folk know everybody's business better than they know it themselves. Everyone knows that Captain Vye had been on a long journey and was tired on the day that he walked back from Anglebury with the reddleman. Grandfer Cantle reports how Wildeve and Thomasin went up the country to 'do the job' at six in the morning. At the village haircutter's it is wondered how Clym can be doing well elsewhere and yet have brought two heavy boxes home. It is harder to keep one's affairs private on Egdon than in London.

Hardy may laugh at the heath-people but he manages to do so without being patronizing. Their way of looking at the world is one that quickly cuts any pretensions down to size – as when they clearly have scant respect for Wildeve's training as an engineer – it has been no use to him at all – or when Clym's attractiveness is enhanced because he is said to belong to a family that had uncommonly long coffins.

Another use of the chorus is in preserving traditional customs. They may not understand these customs, but they honour them through a deep conservatism – simply because things have always been done in a certain way. The mumming play is produced every year without any alteration, and the women make the costumes with pleasing but inappropriate additions, just as they wreathe the maypole in the same way as last year for the Mayday revels. There are similar conventions for the bonfires on old Midsummer night and at the start of November.

Style

By the standards of the twentieth century, Hardy's novels are quite long. This is one of the results of serialized publication, but it is also caused by the public for which they were written, a public that had more leisure than its counterpart today. Reading novels was one of its main entertainments, and what it wanted above all was a good story. This is the main reason why the stylistic drive behind most Victorian novels is a narrative one, and Hardy's novels are typically Victorian in this respect. *The Return of the Native* has a wide variety of different styles within its covers; but what has made it memorable is its imaginative force, a feeling expressed by E. M. Forster when he said 'Hardy seems to me essentially a poet.'

Yet the reader who starts Chapter 1 of the novel might be pardoned if he found it discouraging. The great set description of Egdon Heath has been widely praised and widely criticized; but it does not contain the best of the book. It is written with the painful intensity of close knowledge, and it is important because it sets the tone for the succeeding forty-eight chapters. It uses long words and considerable complexity of grammar – 'an instalment of night', after all, means no more than 'darkness'. It then follows by explaining the same thing in different words: 'darkness had to a great extent arrived hereon while day stood distinct in the sky.' One cannot avoid noticing the self-conscious alliteration, the attempt at balance in the different parts of the sentence, and in 'hereon', a word that was already archaic when it was written. All this is part of the technique of rhetoric. Its list of effects: 'retard the dawn, sadden noon ...' is the first of several similar lists in this chapter, and if rhetoric was, in Hardy's time, an essential tool of anyone destined for a career in public speaking, it had long ceased to be taught in schools; Hardy himself had acquired it through his determined study of the classics.

On the second page we find another characteristic Hardy trait, the use of his huge body of general knowledge to illustrate particular points he wished to make. A large proportion of the textual notes in this volume are written to explain background details that only the most widely read student can be expected to know. Many of these are biblical in origin; many others are classical. Here in this chapter the notes also refer to the *Domesday Book*, the sixteenth-century historian Leland, and various of the European holiday resorts.

The chapter ends in the same manner as Chapter 2 begins – with a road. The author's attention becomes focused on a man walking along it – a favourite Hardy device for starting a novel. After a modicum of description, which covers the two characters involved, he starts for the first time to use direct speech. This is a feature of the whole of *The Return of the Native*. It shows that had Hardy been born at a different time he might well have become a dramatist rather than a novelist, and indeed in his own lifetime many of his novels were turned into plays with his knowledge and encouragement.

All the most effective scenes in the book are presented in this way. One remembers for instance the first meeting between Clym and Eustacia; the gambling for the guineas; the scenes surrounding Mrs Yeobright's last walk; the angry confrontation between Clym and Eustacia. Perhaps the most remarkable use of dialogue, however, lies in the presentation of the rustic chorus. By using it Hardy escapes from the painful and awkward writing that seems to appear whenever he wishes to be really serious; he is able to express a sense of humour that appears nowhere else; and the use of dialect gives a local flavour derived from close observation and intimate knowledge.

Atmosphere

The early part of the book shows great skill in creating atmosphere. It has already been noted how many key scenes take place in darkness; but in each of these the contrasting effect of light in that darkness is equally important. Particularly memorable are the bonfires that spring up all over Egdon, the 'brilliant lights and sooty shades', the metaphors and similes that contrast them, like the 'eye sockets ... deep as those of a death's head', which the flickering fire turns into 'pits of lustre'.

Chapter 3 has a remarkable section devoted to minute observation. The scene where Venn plays Wildeve for the guineas is subtly different, lit with a faint glimmer of lantern light, later to be augmented by thirteen glow-worms, which impart 'a pale phosphoric shine', and it ends 'as the dawn grew visible in the north-east quarter of the heavens'. Different again are the Heath on a frosty night in 2,5, the death of Mrs Yeobright on a warm summer night in 4,8, and the autumnal storm that is a background for 5,8.

Description

Hardy's descriptions of people have a strongly artistic ring about them. Whether he writes about the vivid red that permeated the reddleman, the dark beauty of Eustacia Vye or the intensity that characterizes Clym Yeobright, we are reminded of artistic qualities by the direct mention of painters such as Rembrandt or Dürer, by the search for the striking profile, and by the systematic analysis of the direct effect on the viewer. Eustacia's visual impact constantly confirms features of her character – of the girl who sees herself sentenced to a life on the dark Heath with the lights of Paris periodically and tantalizingly dangled in front of her. The light and shade of her hair, her eyes, her contrasting moods, are as melodramatic as the scenes in which she figures, a feature of the novel which was recognized very soon after it appeared.

The first reviewer of *The Return of the Native* in the *Academy* said 'I know of nothing in later English so striking, and, on the whole, so sound'. D. H. Lawrence wrote at length about the book in 1914, evidently impressed by the imaginative power and the way in which the characters grow out of the landscape that has produced them.

Dialect and directness

Reference has already been made to the use made by Hardy of the rustic chorus. The dialect they use is one of the strongest features of the work. It is easy and natural, and includes several racy Dorset words presented with great skill; for a novelist cannot depart so far from standard English as to make conversations incomprehensible to the average reader from another district. The words he chooses can more often than not be understood in their context. The conversation of his characters is concentrated, to cut out the frequently boring and inconsequential features of real speech. As well as his displays of learning, Hardy shows frequent instinctive use of appropriate and even telling words that are remarkably simple: 'in the slow wind'; 'in the dank dark air'; 'a worn whisper, dry and papery'.

Nature

Of his attention to natural detail there are many examples. The bird life and insect life of the heath; the storm on the summer day, which lacerated the young leaves of trees on the heath; these are written about passionately and are made to fit in with the atmosphere required by the story at that moment. This leads directly to one of the features of Hardy, which he instinctively writes into all his novels: the device known as 'sympathetic background'. To harmonize the weather with the events of a story is an old device, and one can recognize it in stories of young love, which all seem to take place in springtime. For Hardy the key season is late autumn. The novel opens in late November and finishes at the same time of year; we are told that 'the heath had a lonely face suggesting tragical possibilities.'

Symbol

The whole of *The Return of the Native* gathers round Egdon Heath, and makes it into a symbol that enlarges the human situation or attitude into a universal experience. It is a symbol of the unalterable forces of the world, against which man battles in his little life. This story is a very little part of what the Heath has loured and brooded upon since time began. Its dark shape cares nothing for human endeavour and its stubborn soil resists the attempts of man to cultivate it, even as the men upon it are pawns in the game of life. This is stated in the first chapter; it also appears in 5.1:

The imperturbable countenance of the heath, which, having defied the cataclysmal onsets of centuries, reduced to insignificance by its seamed and antique features the wildest turmoil of a single man.

The Heath fits in with the characters of those who have learned to accept it. Eustacia lives in the middle of the Heath and is a lover of wind and storm and night, yet hates it, and so does Wildeve. The likeable characters have no ambition to live anywhere else. Thomasin is a good example. She finds the Heath a ridiculous old place; Venn is absorbed by it and in the roughest weather can find somewhere that will shelter him.

The front of Wildeve's house 'was towards the Heath and Rainbarrow, whose dark shape seemed to threaten it from the sky'. Behind it runs 'a still deep stream'. Eustacia first appears upon the barrow (1,2) where the November wind 'seemed made for the scene, as the scene seemed made for the hour'; the 'mummied heath-bells' were now washed colourless by Michaelmas rains, and gave 'a worn whisper, dry and papery' (1,5). It was symbolic when Clym gave Eustacia his 'pot of bones' from the tumulus and came back from seeing her without noticing the resurrection in nature (3,3). Eustacia accepted Clym with an implied condition, and the light of the moon was hid (4).

When Clym leaves home on account of Eustacia, the trees were now suffering more damage than during the highest winds of winter, and the finch gave up his song. But on the open Heath 'how ineffectually gnashed the storm' and Clym goes home through drizzle. On Clym's wedding morning a sparrow was trapped by the window-glass in Mrs Yeobright's home. Wildeve and Christian Cantle go out on a very dark night, and when Wildeve is playing Venn, it is a 'large death's-head moth' that extinguishes the candle in the lantern. On her way to Eustacia's cottage Mrs Yeobright sat down in the Devil's Bellows, and when the boy left her, 'all visible animation departed from the landscape'. When Clym went to his mother's house some time after the funeral 'a spider had already constructed a large web, tying the door to the lintel, on the supposition that it was never to be used again', and when he got inside, 'the flowers in the window had died through lack of water'.

As Clym goes back to Alderworth with anger in his heart against Eustacia, 'All the life visible was in the shape of a solitary thrush cracking a small snail upon the door-stone for his breakfast.' On the night of the final catastrophe it is a dark night with wind and rain. 'The gloom of the night was funereal; all nature seemed clothed in crepe' (5,7). On the Heath Eustacia was isolated 'from all humanity except the mouldered remains inside the Barrow'. When the tragedy of the story is over and the reader is encouraged to look forward to the future with confidence, Thomasin and Venn marry on a warm day.

Irony

It will have been noticed too that a good deal of this background detail is used to make ironic comments on the events or the characters. The whole scheme of the book reflects Hardy's agnostic and increasingly pessimistic nature at the time the story was written, in that it shows characters who hope that their action will have a particular result, and who live to see a result very different indeed. Thus Clym decides to stay at home, while Eustacia falls in love with him in order that she can live in Paris; his eye trouble makes him poor when she thinks she would, at the very least, be comfortably placed by marrying him. She then finds that Wildeve has become rich. Clym's attempts to study enough to become a teacher result in his damaging his sight. There is much irony, in little comments as well as in the larger scope of the story; as, for instance, when Thomasin is leaving home the second time to be married to Wildeve and, full of misgivings, her aunt says, 'O Tamsie, I don't like to let you go.' As the story falls out, she and Tamsie both have reason to wish that Tamsie had not gone.

Hardy's novels are not particularly subtle. Henry James thought them crude, and his comments on Hardy are patronizing. For all its theatrical qualities, *The Return of the Native* has an intensity of feeling that James never quite matches, for all his subtlety. The book's provincialism is its great strength. It is the first of the line of novels that Hardy wrote where the mood is more tragic than comic, and a worthy precursor to them.

Structure and theme

Structure

The Return of the Native is a clearly structured novel. It is divided into five books of comparable length, followed by a rather shorter epilogue, which was added after pressure from the public. The first of these introduces the three women whose part is as prominent as that of Clym, the Native of the title. It is followed by the introduction of Clym; the third book deals with the flowering of the romance between Clym and Eustacia, the fourth builds up to the arrival of Mrs Yeobright at Alderworth, and the fifth with the direct results of what she sees as her rejection. The whole time-scheme takes a year and a day, and in its emphasis on the orderly sequence of the seasons it can be said to be well balanced. Hardy later said that it was the only one of his novels in which he had obeyed the classical unities of time and place – though he must have known that Aristotle, who is supposed first to have praised these unities, which have had so great an effect on drama over the centuries, did not in fact praise them, but was emphasizing the importance of unity of action.

This balancing of plot is accompanied by a similar balancing of character. Thomasin and Clym both marry against advice. Wildeve and Clym both marry as a gesture, Wildeve of defiance to Eustacia, Clym of defiance to his mother. So it is with the timing of events; on the day that Clym leaves home Thomasin comes back to pay a visit. One partner in each marriage finds attraction elsewhere. Near the start of the story we find Eustacia standing on the Rainbarrow; the book ends with Clym's preaching from the same spot.

The plot of the novel is not without its weaknesses. It is surely improbable that Mrs Yeobright would entrust a huge sum of money to such a person as Christian Cantle. For a woman who had lived on the Heath as long as she had, it is unlikely that she would have chosen to walk six miles across it on the hottest day of the year, when her time is apparently her own. The crucial event of the whole novel depends on a number of coincidences; and if coincidences tend to play a large part in many Hardy novels, here they almost go beyond the bounds of the probable. Mrs Yeobright gets to Clym's cottage just as Wildeve happens to be there on his one visit after Eustacia's marriage. As Eustacia hears Clym stir at the crucial juncture, this makes her think that he is going to answer the door. Johnny Nunsuch happens to be there to see what has happened, though Alderworth is a long way from his home – about five miles. He even sees the face look out of the window, and is on hand a little later to fetch Mrs Yeobright a cup of water. Clym intends to visit his mother that very day – just too late to be of any use; Eustacia goes to her death without seeing Clym's letter waiting for her on the mantelpiece, and without hearing her grandfather's call.

The reddleman, too, takes a strange part in the story. He is uncannily successful in being in the right place at the right time to hear conversations intended to be private – between Wildeve and Eustacia, and Wildeve and Christian Cantle. Eustacia herself overhears conversations between Sam and Humphrey, and later she overhears the mummers talking. These overheard conversations are not the only places where the structure of the story creaks; one might point out other times when events happen because it is convenient for the story that they do so – the meeting of Eustacia and Wildeve at the gipsying in East Egdon, where nobody apparently recognizes them; the almost supernatural arrival of Venn at the Quiet Woman where he tells Thomasin what he has seen; and the capture of a number of adders in the dark.

In the last section Hardy shows a sure instinct for integrating the events with the rest of the story. We first meet Thomasin in Diggory Venn's van as he brings her back from Anglebury. The last appearance of them both is when he carries her home in a dogcart; and it is left to Clym to restore the melancholy tone of much of the story.

Theme

In the same preface in which Hardy wrote about the various heaths, which for the sake of his novel he had combined into one, he suggested that the Heath might have been the setting for the climactic event in the life of a previous king of Wessex – King Lear. In saying this he indicates that tragedy was never far from his mind when he conceived the book. And if it is presumptuous to compare the tragedy of King Lear with that of Clym Yeobright and Eustacia Vye, it suggests that the two works have something in common. At one stage King Lear says while on the Heath in a furious storm 'Pour on; I will endure'; and endurance is one of the themes of *The Return of the Native*. Eustacia has to endure living on a Heath that is torture to her; Clym returns home and finds that soon after he has married the girl of his dreams he is afflicted with failing sight, which seems likely to end up in blindness even before the events that destroy his marriage occur. His stoicism is expressed in a chapter-heading: 'He is set upon by adversities; but he sings a song.' As this suggests, Clym seems actually to enjoy misfortune, and to run headlong to embrace it, when most of the events that befall him are in no way his fault.

This directly leads us into Hardy's philosophy in this, the first of his tragic novels where man's existence is dominated by the force of chance, or fate as it is more frequently called. The deaths of Eustacia, Wildeve and Mrs Yeobright are brought about by fate, and the Clym of the end is a sadly reduced figure from the Native who returned from Paris ten months before. This fate is at best indifferent to all that man tries to do, and at times seems to conspire to frustrate him. Mrs Yeobright's death is largely the result of coincidence; but a fate that causes a girl of twenty to feel that life is not worth living and to commit suicide can only be called cruel.

At the same time, it can be seen that despite all this, there are those who cheerfully survive. Thomasin Yeobright has to suffer a series of accidents and slurs on her reputation that might well cause her to become morose; yet she remains placid, cheerful and uncomplaining. Grandfer Cantle and the company of country-folk are always ready to join in any merrymaking, to look back on times good as well as bad, and to poke fun at one another.

For the whole of Egdon as for Hardy himself, Christianity offers little consolation. The place of the church in the novel is very much on the sidelines. It is a convenient means of celebrating marriages, and the scene of melodramatic episodes such as Mrs Yeobright's forbidding the banns of her niece or Susan Nunsuch's attack on Eustacia with the stocking-needle.

The other festivals are devoid of any religious significance, and one can only speculate on the reasons for the sombre mood that permeates the story. There are comparable scenes in *Far from the Madding Crowd*, but in *The Return of the Native* the tragedy is more unrelieved. Behind it lie Hardy's own loss of faith; the suicide of his great friend Horace Moule at Cambridge; and the increasing strains imposed by his marriage to a woman by no means his intellectual equal, who had ambitions different from his own, and who was less than an unqualified success with his family.

Glossary of dialect words

bagnet Bayonet.
baint Am not.
bang-up Impressive.
beaker Jar.
biding away Keeping away.
billets Logs.
blackheart Whortleberries or bilberries.
clean timber Wood which has had branches and twigs removed.
cleft wood Wood which has been split.
clog Shackle fixed to the foot.
dab Skilled person.
dandy Fine.
dazed Damned.
effets Newts.
fess Lively.
gallicrow Scarecrow.
guisers Mummers.
hare-eyes With protruding or staring eyes.
heling Pouring.
here-right Right here.
huffle Bluster.
jowned Damned, shaken up.
kex Plants with hollow stems which have dried out.
knap Hillock.
mandy Cheeky, saucy.
in mangling In the making.
marnels Marbles.
mart Market.
mollyhorning Messing about.
mommet Terror, a frightening man.
mossel i.e. Morsel.
nammet-time The time of the mid-morning meal taken by agricultural labourers.
numskull Here the skull of the stupid person.
nunny-watch Quandary.
ooser A grotesque wooden mask of a face, used to frighten people.
outstep Out of the way.
overlooked Bewitched, looked over with an evil eye.
racket Noisy party.
rames Skeleton.
ratherripe Early ripe.
rozum away Saw away with the bow.

scammish Rough, clumsy.

scroff Odds and ends, rubbish.

skimmity-riding Skimmington-riding, i.e. a burlesque procession to ridicule an adulterer or a henpecked husband (who in the procession was beaten with a wooden spoon).

slack-twisted Inactive.

slittering Gliding along.

spudding Digging.

stave Song.

strawmote Bit of straw.

stunpoll Blockhead.

tatie digging Potato digging.

to-year This year.

twanky Disgruntled.

upsides with him Better than he.

vell Sign.

vlankers Sparks.

weasand Throat.

wethers Castrated rams.

withywind Convolvulus or bindweed.

zany Fool, buffoon.

General questions

1 'All the characters of *The Return of the Native* are in the grip of obsessions.' Do you agree?

(a) The plot of *The Return of the Native* is relatively straight-forward.
(i) 3 men compete for 2 girls.
(ii) The 'third woman' – Mrs Yeobright – complicates this picture.
(iii) Clym is undone by the struggle that takes place between his mother and Eustacia for his soul – and her obsessive ambition for him.

(b) Eustacia
(i) Her obsession is self-evident – to leave the Heath and go to Paris.
(ii) Irony that the action she takes to bring this about in fact anchors her to it more firmly.
(iii) The man she might have married gains the means to go there first.

(c) Clym
(i) Conceived by Hardy as a missionary – constantly behaves like one.
(ii) Undeviating in his aim – to educate and enlighten.
(iii) Enthusiasm with which he plans i) marriage ii) concentrated study – all to further his ambition.
(iv) Element of selfishness true mark of the zealot.
(v) Redirected later, it makes him blame himself unduly for his mother's death.

(d) Thomasin and Reddleman
(i) Here obsessions are much less. They are more balanced.
(ii) Reddleman's obsession (if it is one) healthy one of marrying Thomasin.
(iii) Wildeve – more superficial character; in love with what he cannot have.
(iv) His restless, philandering nature.

(e) Mrs Yeobright
(i) Uncompromising, puritanical nature likely to produce an obsessive nature.
(ii) In fact her aim – for her son to do well, leave heath.
(iii) This frequent enough not to be called an obsession.

(f) Conclusion
(i) Obsessions are strong features of Clym and Eustacia.
(ii) Elsewhere they are less strong. Perhaps the yardstick of normality is the contented heath-folk rather than the tortured main characters.

2 How far is Eustacia herself to blame for the misfortunes that befall her?

3 Contrast Eustacia and Thomasin as characters.

4 'Hardy's male characters are more complex and less interesting than his female ones.' How far do you agree?

5 Would you agree that the reddleman is a device rather than a real person?

6 How far is the Heath responsible for the events of the novel?

7 What use does Hardy make of the heath-folk in the novel?

8 To what extent does Hardy strain the credulity of the reader by his use of coincidence?

9 'Though the descriptions are uncommonly good, the movement is uncommonly slow.' This sentence is taken from an early review of *The Return of the Native*. How far do you agree with it?

10 How far is Hardy successful in portraying a range of emotions in *The Return of the Native*?

11 Are Hardy's major characters responsible for their own destruction?

12 'Clym Yeobright seems inadequate as a partner for Eustacia Vye.' How far do you agree with this judgement?

13 Consider Hardy as a moralist in *The Return of the Native*.

14 How convincing do you find the conflict between Eustacia and Mrs Yeobright?

15 'In *The Return of the Native*, man is shown as powerless before the force of fate.' Do you agree?

16 'The main weakness of the novel is its plot.' Do you find the plot weak?

17 In what sense can *The Return of the Native* be called a puritan novel?

18 How far does Hardy idealize Egdon Heath?
19 'In a harsh world, Hardy sees man as thirsting for happiness and imagining that he will find it by love in some form or other.' Show how Hardy uses this theme in *The Return of the Native*.

Further reading

The text of the novel

Since the expiry of the copyright in 1978 there have been many editions. The most thorough is still the New Wessex Edition (Macmillan) which as well as Introduction and Notes gives variant readings.

Biography

Hardy, F. E., *The Life of Thomas Hardy 1840–1928* (New Edition Macmillan 1962).

Gittings, Robert, *Young Thomas Hardy* (Heinemann 1975; Penguin 1978). *The Older Hardy* (Heinemann 1978; Penguin 1980).

Williams, Merryn, *A Preface to Hardy* (Longman 1976).

Criticism

Lerner, Laurence and Holmstrom, John, *Thomas Hardy and his readers A Selection of contemporary reviews* (Bodley Head 1968).

Draper, R. P., *Hardy: The Tragic Novels* (Macmillan Casebook series 1975).

Paterson, John, *The Making of* The Return of the Native, (University of California Press 1960).

Gregor, Ian, *The Great Web, The Form of Hardy's major Fiction* (Faber 1974).

Millgate, Michael, *Thomas Hardy, His Career as a Novelist* (Bodley Head 1971).

Pinion, F. B., *A Hardy Companion* (Macmillan 1968).

Vigar, Penelope, *The Novels of Thomas Hardy* (Athlone Press 1974).

Background

Lea, Hermann, *Thomas Hardy's Wessex* (1913 repr. Toucan Press 1969).

O'Sullivan, Timothy, *Thomas Hardy: An Illustrated Biography* (Macmillan 1975).

The Country of 'The Return of the Native' (The Thomas Hardy Society Dorchester 1974) (Leaflet obtainable from Dorset County Museum giving alternative locations for the places mentioned in the novel).